THE TEST OF THE

TRIBAL CHALLENGE

RHINO  TALES

SHEL ARENSON

THE TEST OF THE TRIBAL CHALLENGE

Published by Multnomah Youth
a part of the Questar publishing family

© 1996 by Sheldon Arensen
International Standard Book Number: ISBN: 0-88070-901-4

Cover design: Kevin Keller
Cover illustration: Kenneth Spengler

Printed in the United States of America

For information:
QUESTAR PUBLISHERS, INC.
POST OFFICE BOX 1720
SISTERS, OREGON 97759

Library of Congress Cataloging-in-Publication Data

Arensen, Sheldon.
    The test of the tribal challenge / by Shel Arensen.
      p. cm. — (Rhino tales)
    Summary: Impressed by a Kenyan tribe's coming-of-age ritual, Dean's father
devises twelve "tests of manhood" for his son's twelfth birthday just as a series of
robberies is taking place.
    ISBN 0-88070-901-4 (alk. paper)
    [1. Clubs — Fiction. 2. Robbers and outlaws — Fiction. 3. Fathers and sons —
Fiction. 4. Birthdays — Fiction. 5. Christian life — Fiction. 6. Kenya — Fiction..
7. Mystery and detective stories.] I. Title. II. Series.
PZ7.A683Cas   1996
[Fic] — dc20

                                    96-15683
                                        CIP
                                        AC

96 97 98 99 00 01 02 03 04 05 — 10 9 8 7 6 5 4 3 2 1

To the original Kijabe Tiger Club — Tim, Bill, Jim, and Brad. Thanks

for the enjoyable shared years of childhood in Kenya.

And to my faithful partner in writing fiction — Mwaura Njoroge.

AFRICAN CUSTOMS

"There's one up in that tree," Kamau whispered, easing forward from his crouch behind the shaggy-barked juniper tree. Jon nodded and followed. I stared but couldn't see the pigeon. Kamau balanced the *rungu club* in his hand. It was about two feet long with a baseball-sized knob on the end. I watched fascinated as he twirled it slowly two times. Then he slung the club with all his might. It gave a low, sizzling whistle as it turned end over end, cutting a straight line through the air. It hit some branches in the tree and a fat gray pigeon dropped to the ground followed by a small flurry of cement-colored feathers.

We all ran over. With a smile, Kamau picked up the dead pigeon.

"Wow!" Matt said. "That was cool! You really know how to hurl that club."

Kamau nodded. "I had lots of practice when I used to herd the goats for my father every day. But these days I spend so much time in school. I thought I'd forgotten how to hunt with a club."

We got to know Kamau when he almost died from a mysterious sickness. On one of our hikes we found him and his friend Ngugi crumpled on the ground near their goats. We invited Kamau on a hunt so he could show us his skill with his club. By we, I mean the Rugendo Rhinos. Rhinos is our club name — not our species. The four of us in the Rhinos club are missionary kids who live at Rugendo, a mission station in the Kenya highlands. We're normal American kids growing up in Africa, though I'm not sure the churches we visit in America always think so.

Matt Chadwick is our club captain. He's like a stick of dynamite because he's short, stout and full of energy. His dad teaches at a Bible school training Kenyan pastors.

Dave Krenden built our tree fort in the large sacred fig tree in the forest. He built it so slowly and carefully that it almost drove Matt wild. But when he finally finished the tree house, we all knew it wouldn't come tumbling out of the tree. Dave inherited his building skills from his dad who builds houses for the mission and trains Kenyans in carpentry and masonry. Because he's always careful, Dave is our club treasurer.

Jon Freedman is the youngest member in our club. He loves the bush and can track animals almost as well as a Dorobo hunter. His dad is the doctor at the Rugendo Hospital. Jon doesn't want any responsibilities so he's our club member. Every club has to have some regular members. Ours is Jon.

My name is Dean Sandler. I was born here at Rugendo and think of it as home. My dad works as the editor of a Christian magazine. So the other guys voted me in as secretary even though I get horrible grades in penmanship. Anyway, it's from taking notes at our meetings that I got the idea of writing up some of our adventures. Like the time Matt got kidnapped during our bike safari — but that's another story. And the time we went to the island of Lamu and helped uncover a plot to steal an ancient silver treasure from a ruined Arab city. There was another time when we helped break up a gang of poachers. One thing's for sure — we Rhinos love a good adventure.

As we crowded around and congratulated Kamau on his fine throw, my nose began to run. I was just getting over a cold. I held the outside of my nose with my thumb and index finger and blew hard. My hand filled with mucus, then I shook my fingers with a sharp snapping motion. The nose goop flew into the bushes and then I wiped my hand on the grass.

Kamau looked at me in amazement. "I didn't know you knew how to blow your nose in the proper manner." He stopped and put the knuckle of his index finger into his left nostril and blew the right nostril clear. Then he went on. "My father told me that all you white people have long noses because whenever you have to clear them you take rags and pull hard on your noses. And the worst thing is that when you finish, you put the dirty rag back into your pocket. My father told me when my grandfather first saw a white man stuff the wet rag into his pocket, he threw up."

We all laughed. Matt told Kamau that our parents thought it was disgusting to handle nose mucus with your hands and that's why they used a rag or tissue paper. "But we've grown up here in Africa," Matt said, "and it's a lot easier to use your hand like Dean did. But our noses are still long. I think we're born with long noses. It has nothing to do with our pulling on them."

Kamau smiled. "Many of our customs are different," he said. "But the Bible says we are one in Christ." Then he grew silent and frowned. Finally he asked Matt, "Have you been 'cumcised?"

"What?" Matt asked.

Kamau repeated his question. "Have you been 'cumcised?"

"Oh, I think you mean circumcised," Matt said. "Yes, we were all circumcised when we were babies."

Kamau looked puzzled. "If you were," he paused and then said the next word carefully, "circumcised when you were babies, how do you become men? I'm going to be," again he slowed down to get his pronunciation correct, "circumcised this year with some of my age-mates. We will then be men."

Then he repeated his question. "How will you become men? Surely you didn't become men when you were babies."

We had no real answer. "Maybe when we finish college," Matt said. "Or get married."

"You must be a man before you choose a bride," Kamau said firmly. "You wazungu have some very different customs."

We dropped the subject and hiked home carrying the pigeon. We made a small fire in the cement barbecue at Matt's house and roasted it. The bird didn't have enough meat to satisfy all of us, so Matt brought out a package of hot dogs.

At home that evening I told my dad about our conversation with Kamau. "He says he'll become a man when he's circumcised, Dad."

"That's right," my dad said. "In the Kikuyu tribe when a boy reaches the age of around twelve years, he goes through a rite of passage. In the past the boys had a time of teaching when the elders passed on the traditions of the tribe. They learned how to behave as men. Each family had a special ceremony where the boys were born again. It meant they left childhood behind and started life as an adult. They acted out the birth. There were several tests of physical endurance as well. One was a race through the forest to a certain tree. The one winning the race was looked on as the spokesman for his age group."

"How do you know all this stuff, Dad?" I asked.

"Actually, most of that I read from a book called *Facing Mount Kenya*. A lot of the customs aren't followed too closely anymore. The traditional ceremony ended early in the morning when the young boys went down to the river. Here in the highlands the water gets pretty cold. They stayed in the water up to waist level for almost half an hour to numb their bodies as much as possible. Then each boy sat on a skin with a helper behind him. The circumciser came with his knife and performed the operation. The boys had to sit calmly without wincing or shouting out. It proved their courage. It proved they could be a man."

I cringed and wrinkled my nose. "That sounds like it would hurt!" I said.

"I think it did," my dad said, nodding. "But since the boys

wanted to become men so badly, most of them managed to pass the test. Then special leaves and herbal ointments were used to stop the bleeding. The boys rested until they had recovered, usually about a week. And then they had a celebration because the boys were now men."

I was silent. "Kamau says he's going to be circumcised at the end of the year," I said after a while. "He said he would become a man. Then he asked us something we couldn't answer. He asked us how we became men. How do we American boys become men, Dad?"

"I don't know," he said. "We don't really have a definite time when boys become men." He paused. Then he said, "I wonder..."

"What?" I asked.

"Oh, nothing," he said. Then he walked out of the room.

The next day at school we had choir. The teacher wanted our titchie choir to sing the Kenyan national anthem for the outdoor flag-raising chapel the next week. All of the grade school kids in our school are called titchies — British slang for little kids. Matt sat in the back row and liked to sing in a deep voice. He began in his usual fashion, mocking the teacher about an octave lower than he was supposed to be. Suddenly his voice shot up like the thermometer I'd once dipped into a cup of hot tea to make Mom think I was sick. We all looked in astonishment at Matt. Just as suddenly his voice recovered from its spasm and settled back into a rumble again.

"*Ee Mungu, Nguvu yetu,*" we sang. "Oh God, our strength." Suddenly Matt's voice cracked again. This time it sounded so hilarious that we both started laughing. Matt, who had been balancing his chair on the back two legs, tipped over with a crash.

"What is going on back there?" demanded Miss Farr, our music teacher.

Matt couldn't catch his breath. Finally I managed to stammer, "M-M-Matt's voice cracked. It really sounded funny and I'm sorry we laughed."

Matt had struggled to his feet. "I'm really sorry," he said. But on the word "sorry" his voice did a treble leap again. Neither of us could control our laughter.

"You're both staying after school today," Miss Farr said sternly.

That sobered us up for the rest of the class.

As we walked back up to our classrooms I asked Matt why he'd been goofing around. "I don't know, man," he said. "My voice just began slipping up and down. Usually I can sing low. But today I had no control over what sound came out."

"It sure was weird," I said.

That afternoon after serving my time washing chalkboards for Miss Farr I walked home. When I got there I saw my dad talking to my mom on our front porch as they drank coffee in the late afternoon sun. My mom looked excited. "And here's another idea—" she said, stopping abruptly when she saw me. I saw my dad shut a small red notebook quickly.

"What are you guys talking about?" I asked, helping myself to a chocolate chip cookie made with big chunks cut from a Cadbury's dark chocolate bar instead of tiny American chocolate chips.

"Us?" my dad asked innocently. "Oh, nothing."

chapter two

BIRTHDAY PARTY AT LAKE NAIVASHA

That night after supper my dad asked what I wanted to do for my birthday celebration. I would turn twelve in a few weeks. I thought for a minute before answering. "I'd like to have my party at Lake Naivasha. We could have a picnic at Fisherman's Camp and even go fishing."

My parents looked at each other. "Sounds good to me," Mom said.

"And can I invite the other Rhinos, and Kamau?" I asked.

Dad nodded. "Sure," he said. "It might be a bit crowded, but that would be fine. Your birthday's on a Friday, so how about if we have the party on Saturday. We could go over early, do some fishing, have the party—"

"Why can't we go over Friday night and camp overnight?" I asked. "Then we could have more time for fishing."

My dad checked his calendar. "Looks okay," he said. "I'll just have to check with the other parents to see if they'll give their permission."

Everyone got permission to go. I could hardly wait until my birthday weekend. After school on that Friday, I ran home to help my parents pack. My little brother Craig had packed all his things inside our old blue sleeping bag and he sat on it next to the Land Rover, ready to go. I went in and carried out the cooler full of food. Dad had already packed the tents, camp chairs and fishing equipment on the roof rack.

Soon Matt arrived followed by Jon and Dave. They each carried their own sleeping bags. Matt pulled a slightly bent envelope out of his pocket. "I can't wait," he said. "And besides, it's your birthday today." Inside was a birthday card with a giraffe on the front. The other guys often called me *twiga*, the Swahili word for giraffe, because I was taller than anyone else. "Open it," Matt urged. I did and a twenty-shilling note fell out. I reached down and picked up the blue money with the picture of Kenya's president on one side. Twenty shillings is about fifty cents in American money.

"Thanks, Matt," I said. "I'm sure I can think of a good way to spend this."

Dave and Jon said they'd give me their presents later.

My dad asked for some help tying down the load on top. Jon scrambled up and criss-crossed a rope back and forth across the old gray tarp that covered the luggage. Dad cinched it down and tied it off. "All right, get in," he said. "We're set to go." Craig had already climbed in between the two front seats. No one fought with him over that seat because he had to straddle the gear shift.

"Wait," I said, "Kamau's not here yet."

My dad thought for a moment. "Well, let's drive over by his house. Are you sure you told him it was today?"

"Yes," I answered.

"And the time?" he went on.

"Yes, I did. And Kamau said he'd be here."

We drove across the mission station to where Kamau's family had a small farm. I could see Kamau sitting in front of his house. "Come on, it's time to go," I called.

Kamau didn't answer. I got out and went over to ask him what was going on. Finally Kamau said, "I can't come."

"Why not?" I asked.

"I don't have a sleeping bag like all the rest of you," he said. "My mother told me just to take a blanket. But I didn't want to be different."

I felt terrible. I hadn't even thought Kamau would be embarrassed because he didn't have a sleeping bag. "It's okay," I said. "You can borrow mine."

He looked at me. "Are you sure? What about you, then? Where will you sleep?"

I thought of Craig packing an adult-sized sleeping bag. I took a deep breath. "I can sleep with my brother. He has a big sleeping bag."

Kamau smiled. His white teeth contrasted sharply with his dark skin and we got into the Land Rover.

After an hour's drive we arrived at Fisherman's Camp. We pitched the tents under some large yellow fever trees, then my dad announced, "There's just enough time for a quick fishing trip. The large-mouth bass in this lake like to bite in the late afternoon. Who wants to come?"

Mom and Craig stayed in camp to get supper started. The rest of us helped carry lures and poles out to the narrow wooden dock which floated on empty metal fifty-gallon fuel drums. As Kamau stepped on the dock, which dipped and swayed under our weight, his eyes shot open and he grabbed me by the arm, almost knocking me over the side.

"Move aside, boys," Dad said. He brushed past us carrying the outboard motor to the small aluminum boat our family kept at the lake. As he stepped in and began attaching it to the back of the boat, I tried to walk forward and put my gear in. But Kamau wouldn't release his grip on me.

"I can't swim," he said desperately. "I'm afraid of the water."

I told him he could stay on the shore but he said he didn't want to be left behind.

"Matt," I said, "bring me one of those orange life vests." We always carried enough for each passenger. Prying Kamau's grip off my arm, I fastened the life vest on him and tightened it. "Now," I explained, "if you fall in the water, just lie on your back and this will keep you floating and we'll help you get back to shore." Kamau nodded and took a deep breath before stepping into the boat.

My dad pulled a few times on the starter rope, then adjusted the choke throttle before the motor started with a thumping roar. He turned the boat neatly and we pulled into the open lake.

"We won't have time to get all the way to Hippo Point and back before dark," he shouted over the roar of the motor.

"I'll just head up along the shore aways and we'll troll along the edge of the papyrus. Dean, can you get a couple of lines ready? We'll only use two poles for now or the lines will get tangled. You boys will just have to take turns."

I connected the poles, threaded the line, and then attached a lure to the swivel hook on the end of each line. For one pole I chose a milk chocolate brown Rapala plug with a golden belly. I gave it to Matt.

"I want to use that lure there," Jon said pointing at a zebra-striped Pico Perch.

"We haven't had much luck with that lure," Dad said, looking over my shoulder into the lure box. "But give it a try. You never know. And watch out for hippos. If your line catches a hippo, drop the pole or break the line. I don't want to have an angry hippo coming after the boat."

"You're kidding, aren't you, Mr. Sandler?" Matt asked.

My dad raised his eyebrows and we couldn't tell if he was kidding or not.

Soon Matt and Jon had dropped their lures in the water and let out quite a bit of line. Dad slowed down to trolling speed. Kamau's fingers were glued to the edge of the boat. He tried to smile.

Suddenly Matt's pole bent double and the drag began to click. "I've got something!" he shouted, reeling in his line like crazy.

"Is it a fish?" my dad asked, shutting off the motor and reaching for the dip net.

"I think so," Matt said. But as the boat slowed, it looked like whatever was on Matt's line was not pulling back. He kept reeling in. But when the lure came to the surface, Matt saw that he'd hooked a wad of reeds off the bottom of the lake.

Dad chuckled. "Pull the weeds off and let's try again," he said, starting the motor.

Matt handed the rod to me. I asked Kamau if he wanted to try. He shivered, looking miserable as he held onto the side of the boat. "No thank you," he said softly. I tossed the line over and watched it unravel over the reel. When I felt I'd let out enough line I turned the handle on the spinning reel one time until it clicked. Then I held it gently, feeling for a bite.

Suddenly I felt a tug. I gave a quick twitch on the pole but said nothing. I didn't want to have a false alarm like Matt. Then I felt an extra sharp pull followed by a jerk. I knew I had a fish. "Slow down, Dad, I think I've got something," I said as I started reeling in the line. Dad cut the motor and watched as I kept the end of my pole up and worked the fish closer to the boat. About ten yards away the bass leaped, making a big splash in the water. But I kept the line tight and soon Dad slipped the net underneath the fish and dropped it into the boat.

The fish flipped back and forth. Dad reached in and held it firmly with one thumb in its mouth and his fingers under the lower jaw. He pulled out the hook and held the fish up. "Not bad, Dean," he said. "That's about a three-pound bass. It'll make a good meal tonight."

He put it in our metal fish cage and dropped it over the side. We trolled for about another twenty minutes with no more success.

"Let's go home, boys," my dad said. We pulled in the fish cage and we headed back to camp.

I helped Kamau out of the boat. He walked unsteadily off the dock. "Did you like the boat ride?" I asked.

He looked at me uncertainly. "I'm glad I did it," he said. "My friends will never believe me when I tell them." He smiled and I could tell he felt a lot better with his feet on grass.

Jon asked my dad if he could fillet the fish. We watched him make a cut down the fish's back and then down right along the rib cage, cutting the slab of meat free just above the belly. The pinkish-white fish meat still had the skin on one side. Jon flipped the fish over and sliced out another fillet. Then he made a V-shaped slice to remove a few bones near the center front of each piece of meat before washing his hands off in the lake.

We took the fish fillets up to where Dad had a fire started. Mom had supper already cooked on a small cookstove. The campfire was for roasting our fish. We took a special barbecue sauce my dad had made at home and gobbed some on the fish. We laid a small metal grill on the fire between three stones. When the fire burned down to red coals, we put the fish flesh side down on the grill. It sizzled for about a minute. Then we flipped the fish over with a spatula so it was skin down to the fire. The white fish had black lines scorched across it from the grill. We sprinkled salt and more barbecue sauce on it and let it cook slowly over the fire while we ate our supper, a beef stew that Mom had made at home. She also brought out big loaves of homemade bread which we broke into pieces to dip in the stew.

As we finished, my dad said the fish looked ready. We ate the delicious meat right out of the charred skin. It tasted wonderful. Even Kamau tasted some. "Now I know why the

Luo like fish," he said. "Usually we Kikuyu never eat fish and we laugh at the Luo, who live on Lake Victoria, for eating so much fish."

We did the dishes as a team using water warmed over the fire. Then we sat around the campfire. My dad went into his tent and brought back a package that had been neatly wrapped by my mom.

"Since it is your twelfth birthday today, we thought we'd give you a special gift. Something we've never done before," he began. It sounded like he was starting a sermon so I settled back in the chair.

"You asked me a few weeks ago how American boys became men," he continued.

Just then from under the trees a very large gray shape appeared walking straight towards our camp!

chapter three

DEAN'S TWELVE
TASKS OF
MANHOOD

The shape stopped moving and a ripping, tearing sound erupted, like someone pulling open a Velcro fastener. "Everyone sit absolutely still," Dad ordered.

I had a terrible urge to run to the outhouse. "It's a hippo," my dad whispered as the shape edged closer to our tents and the yellow glow of our kerosene lamp. "It's come up out of the water to feed and it's eating grass. If we don't move it will pass on by."

I could just make out the shape of the hippo's head as it continued tearing up large mouthfuls of grass near our tents. I tried not to breathe too loudly. Then, just as Dad had predicted, the hippo meandered away from our campsite, munching as it walked.

"That hippo's huge!" Jon said.

"He's even bigger than Beasley the hippo in my picture book about the bigness contest!" Craig said in a tiny, awed voice.

"Yes," my dad said. "Hippos are very large. And they can be lethal, too. They look so jolly and plump waddling around eating grass. But they have long tusks that can crunch a person in half."

Kamau shivered and said, "I don't like hippos at all."

"Usually they don't bother people," my dad said, "unless someone gets in between them and the water. They feel very insecure when someone cuts them off from their escape route to the water."

"Like Craig and I did by accident at Mzima Springs," I said. My brother and I had stumbled onto a hippo once before and knew how dangerous they could be.

Just then we saw a flashlight beam. It was the guard for the campsite. The hippo's eyes gleamed crazily in the light. *"Wee, toka!"* the guard said. "You, get out of here!"

The hippo dropped his head and trundled away across the grass, disappearing into the lake with a splash.

"Well, that was exciting," my dad said, getting up and pushing a few more logs into our campfire. "Now, Dean, why don't you open your present."

I looked down at the package on my lap. The wrapping paper was crumpled where I had been gripping it tightly as we watched the hippo. I ripped open the paper and pulled out a big book. "Thanks Mom and Dad," I said. "What's the book about?"

"Look closer," Mom said.

I examined the book and saw it was a photo album. "Pictures?" I asked.

"Just read it," Dad said.

I opened up the photo album. On the first page was a hand-drawn title which read: *Dean Sandler's Twelve Tasks of Manhood.*

"Twelve Tasks of Manhood?" I questioned. "What's this all about?"

"Read on," my dad said.

On the next two pages my parents had each written a letter telling me I was just beginning to enter manhood. They told me the years ahead when I was a teenager might be hard with a lot of changes. And in preparation they prayed and came up with a list of twelve tasks which I had to accomplish before my next birthday so I could become a man. Some would challenge me to grow in my spiritual life as a Christian. Some would challenge me physically. Others mentally.

"Well, tell us what you have to do," Matt said impatiently.

I wasn't sure I wanted to know. I thought of my talk with my dad about the Kikuyu traditional circumcision.

"Yes, tell us what you have to do to become a man," Kamau said, sitting up on the edge of his camp chair.

The next page of the book was almost all blank. At the top my mom had written: Task One. You shall run thirty miles in thirty days.

"Hey, I can do that," I said. "That's just a mile a day for one month."

My dad said, "We've left the pages mostly blank so we can take pictures of you doing each task. Then we can put the pictures or something that shows you've completed the task.

Then you'll have the book to remind you of the time you became a man. Kind of like the memorial stones the Israelites set up near the Jordan River."

I read the next one. Task Two. You shall memorize the book of Colossians.

"Mom," I complained, "I'll never be able to memorize that much."

She smiled. "Yes, you can. I know you've never memorized a section that long before, but I know you can. It will help you understand Colossians as well as teaching you to meditate on God's Word." Trust my parents to turn a fun twelfth birthday party into a spiritual lesson.

I turned the page. Task Three. You shall camp out in the forest overnight all by yourself.

"You're so lucky, Dean!" Jon exclaimed. "A camp-out!" I liked the camp-out part, too. It was the "all by yourself" phrase that made my stomach churn. But I didn't dare admit it. Instead I swallowed hard and said, "Yeah, I can't wait to do that one."

I read on.

Task Four. You shall read the books from the following reading list. *Things Fall Apart* by Chinua Achebe, *The River Between* by Ngugi wa Thiong'o, Isaiah from the Bible, *The Cross and the Switchblade* by David Wilkerson, *Tortured for Christ* by Richard Wurmbrand, *Cry, the Beloved Country* by Alan Paton, *Facing Mount Kenya* by Jomo Kenyatta, *The Lion, the Witch and the Wardrobe* by C.S. Lewis. I loved to read so this task looked okay to me.

Task Five. You shall play a round of golf with your dad.

"Can I really go golfing with you, Dad?" I asked. I'd only gone to the golf course near Nairobi once. I had acted as my dad's fore caddy which meant standing up on the fairway dodging the drives and trying to remember where the golf balls landed. I'd spent the day in fear of being tagged on the noggin with a golf ball. But to be able to play a round!

"Yes," my dad said. "I think you're old enough to play a round of golf."

I turned back to the book. Task Six. You shall do a Bible study on Daniel.

"How do I do that?" I asked.

My mom smiled, "I've got a study for you. It will teach you how to read the Bible and understand it for yourself."

Task Seven. You shall spend three days with the Njoroge family on their farm near Nakuru.

"What will I do there?" I asked. Mr. and Mrs. Njoroge were the parents of my dad's editor at the magazine. We had visited their farm a number of times, but only for a meal.

"You'll help them with chores around the farm," my dad said. "And find out how a Kenyan family lives."

Task Eight. You shall climb to the top of Fischer's Tower in Hell's Gate.

"Fischer's Tower?" I asked. "How am I supposed to climb to the top? It's steep!"

"One of the new missionaries at Rugendo is a rock climber," Dad said. "He's agreed to teach you how to climb it."

"With ropes and things?" I asked.

My dad nodded.

"You're so lucky, Dean," Matt said. He and Jon looked at the page longingly the way our dog gazed at my plate whenever we ate barbecued meat on our front porch. Matt and Jon loved to clamber up any cliffs we found on our hikes. I usually looked for an easy way around.

Task Nine. You shall prepare and serve a complete meal for four at your own restaurant.

Mom explained, "You know how sometimes you and Craig have pretended at home that we're eating at a restaurant? Well, this is your chance to come up with your own restaurant and invite some guests."

"I hope you invite us!" Matt said.

Task Ten. You shall attend a soccer camp and sharpen your soccer skills.

"I'd love to do this, Dad," I said, "but there aren't any soccer camps in Kenya."

"Sure there is," he said. "I'm holding it and all your friends are invited to join in."

"All right!" Matt said, speaking for everyone.

Task Eleven. You shall climb to Point Lenana on top of Mt. Kenya.

"Mt. Kenya!" I exclaimed. "I get to climb Mt. Kenya?"

"Yes," Dad said. "I think you're old enough and strong enough to make the climb."

"When can we go?" I asked.

"It may be a while, so slow down. Work on the other tasks first and we'll organize the climb up Mt. Kenya towards the end of the year. And after you finish that one you can do your final task in the book."

I looked at the last page. Task Twelve. You shall eat a giant all-the-meat-you-can-eat meal at the Carnivore Restaurant in Nairobi.

"I can't believe it," I said, shutting the book gently. "What a way to celebrate my twelfth birthday. It'll take most of the year."

"It's meant to," Dad said. He put his arm around my shoulder. "You're growing up. And we want you to remember the year you became a man."

After Dad told some stories and we sang songs under the stars, we headed to our tents. Craig had fallen asleep in Dad's arms so he told me just to take the old blue sleeping bag. Craig could sleep with Mom and Dad.

I gave my sleeping bag to Kamau and we all snuggled in, whispering and joking.

Matt punched me in the arm. "Man, you sure are lucky," he said. "Climbing Mt. Kenya, eating at the Carnivore, camping out alone." Then he paused. "Actually some of those things are pretty hard. Memorizing the whole book of Colossians. And that reading list. I'd never be able to sit down and read all those books."

I laid awake for a long time thinking about the book. Yes, some of the tasks looked like fun. But some scared me. I wondered if Kamau and the other Kikuyu boys ever felt scared before being circumcised. I prayed and asked God to help me complete my twelve tasks of manhood.

The next morning we went fishing again after breakfast and we each caught a couple of bass. When we got back to camp, Mom said it was time for my birthday cake. She took the cake out of a plastic sealed container. It was shaped like a rocket ship. "It looks great, Mom." I especially liked the thick frosting that covered the top.

Mom set the cake on an old tree stump and then added the final touch. She poked some sparklers into the back of the cake and lit them instead of candles. It looked like the rocket ship was taking off with blazing jet engines. They sang "Happy Birthday" to me and I tried to blow out the sparklers. I couldn't and everyone teased me about how many girlfriends I had. We let them burn out and then Mom cut the cake.

As we sat in the grass eating cake and drinking Cokes, Jon sniffed a few times. Then he looked at the stump. "Hey," he said, "the stump is smoking!"

"You're right," my dad said. "It's on fire!" He went over to look. Then he laughed. "It looks like some of the hot pieces of sparkler fell into the stump and it's on fire." We poured water down the stump but it continued to smolder.

By the time we had taken down our camp, the stump was still smoking. We apologized to the campsite owner and he laughed. "It's been in the way for years. I've just been too lazy to pull it out," he said. "Now it looks like you've figured a way to burn it out for me."

We stopped in town so my mom could buy some elephant ears at the Bell Inn. I don't mean real elephant ears, but that's what we called the flaky pastries made specially by the baker at the Inn. As we sat in the car waiting, I looked down a row of small wooden shops called kiosks. Some sold fish, others sold fruit and vegetables. And I saw one that had some greenish twigs tied in bundles hanging across the window of the kiosk. A hand-painted sign read: Fresh *miraa*.

"What's *miraa*?" I asked.

"Who knows?" Matt answered. "Look, there's your mom coming now."

We drove up the steep bank on the edge of the Rift Valley for about an hour until we arrived back at Rugendo. We dropped off the other guys at their homes.

"Thanks for inviting me," Kamau said. "And for letting me use your sleeping bag."

"You're welcome," I answered.

My dad pulled into our driveway and unlocked the door to the house. As we stepped in we saw papers and clothing strewn all over the floor.

"Oh no!" Dad said. "We've had a break-in!"

chapter four

BREAK-INS

Craig started crying and my mom picked him up.

"Wait here," Dad said. Picking up my old baseball bat he cautiously walked farther into the house.

"There's no one down here," he said, coming back and starting up the stairs. Then he disappeared out of sight. "Well, here's how they got in," we heard him call. "Come on up. Whoever broke in has gone."

We walked up the stairs, tiptoeing over the debris. "My monkey!" Craig cried out, trying to reach down and pick up his stuffed toy which lay sprawled on top of a pile of my dad's bank statements.

"Be careful, Craig!" Mom said sharply. "You almost knocked me off the stairs."

I picked up the monkey and gave it to him. Craig hugged it to his chest.

Once upstairs I saw a gaping hole in the roof. Dad examined it. "They pried off one of the corrugated asbestos roofing sheets," he said poking his head out of the hole and looking outside. "I can see the marks where they climbed onto the roof over the carport. And it looks like they used our old *jembe* (garden hoe) as the tool to pull the roof up." The rusty hoe lay on the floor underneath the hole in the roof.

I popped my head through the hole and saw the broken roofing sheet in the flowers. It looked like a ridged potato chip that had been broken and dropped.

"Oh no!" my mom called as she looked into their bedroom. "They've taken all my clothes from the closet! And all my shoes!"

Dad walked over and put his arm on her shoulder. "It feels like someone has invaded our innermost place," she said, starting to sob.

My dad held her for a few minutes. Then he said we should thank the Lord that nobody had gotten hurt. "They've taken a lot of things," he said. "We'll have to make a list to give to the police. But things can always be replaced." He looked at us. "I have all of you and that's what really matters."

We prayed and then began picking up the mess. My mom made a list of things that were missing and my dad tried to get the police on the phone. They said they could come if he drove down and got them. Otherwise they had no transportation and couldn't come.

My dad shook his head in exasperation. "I guess I'd better go get them. I doubt they'll catch anyone, but if some of the items do show up in the used market, they might be recovered." He paused. "Though I doubt that as well. But we have to report the break-in."

As he walked out, he slipped on some books and papers strewn across the floor. Catching his balance, he reached down and picked up four small blue books. "Our passports," he said. "Well, at least they didn't take those." He put them on top of the dresser. "What a mess," he murmured before he drove off to get the police.

When we had finally cleaned up, it appeared that we'd lost a pair of binoculars, a tape recorder, a radio, shoes, and lots of clothes.

Our break-in was the talk of Rugendo the next day at church. "I think one of the thieves only had one leg," I told the other Rhinos who had crowded around to ask what had happened.

"Why do you say that?" Dave asked.

"Because in my closet they stole three shoes. All three were the left foot of a pair. So now I've got three right shoes without any left shoe to match. Mom says that if she sees a one-legged man she's going to check if he's wearing my shoes!"

We all laughed.

We walked by Matt's house on our way home from church. Jon looked up at Matt's window. "Did you break your window with a soccer ball?" he asked.

"No, why?" Matt said, puzzled.

"It's broken," Jon said, pointing.

"What? You're right!" Matt said, going over. "It looks like it was broken with a rock. And—Hey! Someone took my radio! I kept it on top of this shelf."

Broken glass littered the floor of his room and a fist-sized rock lay in the middle of the glass.

"Someone broke the window with that rock and walked off with your radio," Dave said.

"This is crazy!" Matt said, running back to church to tell his dad what had happened.

Our home was the first one broken into. But it wasn't the last. Over the next month other homes were burglarized. Most often windows were broken and the thieves grabbed whatever was within reach. Other times people lost clothes from the clotheslines that we string out behind our homes to dry our clothes. And it wasn't only missionaries who were losing things. Kamau's father lost several of his tools while his family was at a prayer meeting at church. The pastor's son had his bicycle stolen.

But though the police were called in, they couldn't seem to find who was doing all the stealing.

Everyone at Rugendo became suspicious of everyone else. "This is really bad," my dad said one evening at supper. "Suspicion ruins relationships. A young man came to our office today asking for some part-time work. Right away Mr. Njogu and I wondered if he was somehow involved in this burglary epidemic. We did a background check and what do you think we found out? He's a strong Christian who has worked for some other missionaries since he was a boy. His wife is having a difficult pregnancy and she has to stay at our hospital for a few months. He's just trying to get some work while he's here waiting. I felt so bad suspecting him that we decided to give him a job wrapping magazines."

Then the stealing trickled to a halt. No one knew for sure

why it stopped. Everyone was less suspicious. But we'd learned not to leave things next to windows.

With all the break-ins, I'd nearly forgotten about my list of twelve tasks. I started reading some of the books, but I knew I'd have to get busy on the difficult items if I was going to complete them all before a year went by.

"Can I do my overnight camp-out?" I asked. "This weekend would be a good time."

Dad scratched his chin as he thought. "Yeah, I think that would be okay. Now, you'll have to plan your own meals — supper and breakfast. You'll have to carry your gear out alone, set it up, and spend the night alone. Think you can handle it?"

"I'm not sure it's such a good idea," Mom said. "With all the stealing that's been going on, I don't know if I want him out there alone."

My dad thought again. Then he said to her, "You're right. It is a risk. Whoever has been doing the stealing seems to have left the area. But it's still a risk. Really, though, that's what a challenge like this is all about for Dean. Maybe we can come up with a compromise."

"Does this mean I don't have to sleep out by myself?" I asked, trying to hide my relief.

"No," he said. "Since we live on the edge of the forest, I think we could pick a site that is far enough from the house for you to feel like you're all alone. But it would still be close enough for you to signal for help if something did happen. I'll give you one of the security air horns that we bought when all the burglaries began."

Our plan suited my mom. I couldn't back out of it now. Dad and I walked into the forest and checked out some possible sites. We found a small opening behind some thick thorn bushes where I could fit the small dome tent. And it was out of sight of our house and completely surrounded by forest.

On Saturday I got ready. I packed hot dogs and bread that I would cook over a small campfire. I poured water into an army-style canteen and hooked it to my utility belt. For breakfast I'd have cold cereal. I filled a plastic bowl with my mom's homemade granola and popped a lid on the bowl, along with a small box of some Safariland milk. Snacks included oranges, candy bars, two bottles of Coke, and *mandazi,* square Kenyan doughnuts. Then I collected my sleeping bag, pillow, and the tent. I dropped the air horn, a flashlight, a hatchet, and a box of matches in my backpack.

"Think you have everything?" Dad asked.

"I think so," I said.

He helped me lift the backpack onto my shoulders. Then he took a picture and handed me my Bible before I walked to my campsite. "You might get lonely and want something to read," he said.

I set up the tent first. It was late afternoon so I gathered sticks and started my campfire. I roasted my hot dogs and drank a Coke as the sun dropped behind the trees.

Then it was dark. I huddled next to the fire for a while, eating a candy bar. I thought of something I'd forgotten. A toothbrush.

As night settled around me like thick fog during the rainy season, I listened to the sounds around me. The piercing squeak of cicadas, insects that live in trees, filled the forest. In the distance I heard the *eee-yonk* call of a blue monkey. "I wonder if the monkeys are trying to get away from a leopard?" I said out loud.

I shivered. I dumped some dirt on my dying campfire and got into the tent. Using my flashlight I read from Psalm 70. "Hasten, O God, to save me; O Lord, come quickly to help me...You are my help and my deliverer; O Lord, do not delay."

I said a quick prayer asking God to deliver me from any dangers. Then I snuggled into my sleeping bag. But it was too early to go to sleep. I decided to start my task of memorizing the book of Colossians. But before I'd gotten past the first verse my flashlight began to dim. The light turned to a dull orange. I turned it off, hoping the batteries might recover and give me more light later if I needed it.

I lay in the dark of the tent and listened. I fingered the air horn that I'd placed next to the sleeping bag.

Then I heard a shriek. I sat up, panting with fear. The sound came again. This time I recognized it. "It's only a bush baby," I said to myself. I forced myself to put my head down. A bush baby is a monkey-like animal with eyes as big as pogs. The first Europeans in Africa had called them bush babies because their nighttime call sounded like a baby crying out in the forest. I whispered another prayer to God asking for courage.

I guess I finally drifted off to sleep because I suddenly woke up to the sound of running feet right outside my tent!

chapter five

ROCK CLIMBING

I reached for the air horn and squeezed the trigger. The sharp blast drowned out the sound of a voice outside the tent.

Then I heard my name. "Dean! Dean! Are you all right?" It was Dad!

"Yes, I'm fine," I said fumbling in the dark to open the tent zipper. I fell into my dad's arms.

"Why did you hit your air horn?" he asked.

"I heard someone crashing through the forest and it woke me up. Why did you come down here? Is something wrong at home?"

Dad frowned. "Now I'm confused," he said. "I came running down here when I heard your air horn."

"But I didn't hit my air horn until a minute ago when I heard you running through the bushes."

"Are you sure?"

"Yes, I'm sure," I answered.

Just then we heard the piercing blare of another air horn and the sound of someone shouting. A dog began to bark ferociously. "That noise is coming from over at the Richardsons' house!" my dad said. "I'll bet the air horn I heard at first came from their house. I woke up from a deep sleep from the sound of an air horn and all I could think of was you. Come on, let's get you back to the house. Something's going on at the Richardsons' place, and I don't want to leave you down here by yourself. We can pick up your stuff in the morning."

I hustled behind my dad, scraping my leg on some thorns as we pushed our way through the bushes. When we threw open the door to our house, Mom stood there in her pink robe. "Thank you Lord," she breathed when she saw me. "I would never have forgiven myself if something had happened to you."

"Dean's fine," Dad said. "It wasn't even his air horn we heard. But there's some commotion going on over at the Richardsons'. Lock the house. I'm going over to see what's happening." He opened the door, then turned back. "And pray!"

Mom and I sat down on the couch and she began to pray for safety for the Richardsons and for my dad. I prayed, too. Then she asked if I'd like some hot cocoa. We walked into the kitchen and I watched her mixing the milk, cocoa powder, and sugar in a large pan.

"Were you scared in the forest by yourself?" she asked.

"Kind of," I admitted. "I read a verse from Psalm 70 and it

helped me know God was my helper and my deliverer. A bush baby kept me awake for awhile. Once I fell asleep I had no problem until I heard Dad running up to my tent. Then I about had a heart attack."

The cocoa began to boil and Mom pulled it off the gas stove and poured a cup for me. "We were scared when we heard an air horn go off. I heard it first. I hadn't been able to sleep at all with you all alone in the forest. I woke your dad and told him to get down to your tent right away."

Mom reached into the cupboard and pulled out a bag of marshmallows. They had been sent out from one of our churches in the States as part of a package of goodies. Mom had told them that marshmallows worked well as padding and then we'd have a treat as well. Unfortunately the long, hot boat journey had left the marshmallows all melted into one puffy white mass. She ripped off a chunk the size of a golf ball and popped it into my cup of cocoa.

As we sat sipping the cocoa Dad came back. His face looked tight and worried. "What happened?" Mom asked.

He looked at me briefly. "I guess you're old enough to listen," he said. "Some thugs broke into the Richardsons' house while they were sleeping. One of them picked up a fish tank thinking it was a television. It was too heavy and he set it back down hard enough to wake the Richardsons. When Sam walked in to see what the noise was, one of the robbers hit him over the head with a *panga* knife.

"Then they ran away. Mrs. Richardson hit the air horn. By the time I got there, Dr. Freedman had already examined the gash on Sam's forehead. Dr. Freedman stopped the bleeding and then took Sam over to the hospital for stitches."

"What about Mrs. Richardson?" I asked.

"She was still crying, so Mrs. Freedman took her over to spend the night with them." Dad paused. "We decided this has gone too far. We're going to have a station meeting tomorrow with the church leaders and the police to discuss security." Then he led us in prayer.

I looked at my cup of cocoa. Now it was cold. I ate the melted marshmallows off the top, but they didn't taste very good. The violent break-in at the Richardsons' had put a sour taste in my mouth.

The next morning Dad helped me carry my camping gear back up to the house. "I think we'll consider this task complete," he said. "Even if you didn't spend the whole night in the forest alone, you faced a scary night." Then he took a picture of me folding up the tent.

That day the missionaries and church leaders held their security meeting. Dad told us about it at supper. The police couldn't offer more help because they didn't have enough policemen in the area. So the missionaries and church leaders decided to do three things. First, they prayed God would protect all the residents at Rugendo. And they gave thanks for Mr. Richardson who was recovering from the cut on his head. Second, the station decided to put iron gates on the doors and bars on the windows of all the houses on the station. Third, the men agreed to volunteer to patrol the station at night.

"We divided the night from 10 P.M. to 6 A.M. into two four-hour shifts," Dad said. "We'll have two cars with two men in each car and we'll drive around the station. Quite a few of the Kenyan men also volunteered, so we only have to go on patrol two, sometimes three nights a week. I'm on tonight with Pastor Waweru from ten o'clock to two in the morning."

In the weeks that followed, the patrols and iron gates and bars stopped the break-ins.

"I don't like all these new bars," Matt said at our supper table one evening. I'd invited him over to eat Swedish pancakes, my dad's specialty. Dad, who stood at the stove pouring pancake batter into a black frying pan, heard Matt's comment.

Leaning his head back, Dad said, "It's kind of like being in a prison, isn't it?"

"Yes," Matt answered. "Even with the curved design of the bars in the windows, it still feels like a prison."

"It's given people more peace of mind. And it makes it harder for anyone to break in," Dad said. "Though they could always break through the roof like they did at our house. No security system will stop a determined burglar from breaking in. Actually, I think the greatest thing that's happened has been the praying that goes on while the men are on patrol. Somehow, being out at night makes us realize we need God's help."

He took a spatula and flipped a plate-sized pancake. "And I think it's because of our prayers that the burglaries stopped." He yawned. "But some nights I wish I didn't have to be on patrol. I miss my sleep."

He brought in a plate heaped with tortilla-thin pancakes. I showed Matt how to put a gob of butter in the middle and then spoon a thick line of chunky sugar on the pancake. Then I showed him how to roll it up like a burrito and eat it. Matt copied me and took a bite. "This is great, Mr. Sandler," he said.

Dad finished making the pancakes and joined us at the table. As he prepared his pancake, he said, "I forgot to tell you, Dean. Mr. Jenkins said he could climb Fischer's Tower with you on Saturday." I felt a chill. I really didn't like heights and this task was one I'd kind of wished might be forgotten during the year. I think my dad knew that and that's why he'd arranged for Mr. Jenkins to take me.

Dad looked at Matt. "If any of you Rhinos want to go along, Mr. Jenkins said that after he and Dean climb to the top of the tower, he'll come down and teach anyone else who's interested in basic climbing techniques at Hell's Gate."

"You mean we can do some climbing, too? I'm sure all the other guys will want to go!" Matt said.

On Saturday we drove out to Hell's Gate, a volcanic gorge near Lake Naivasha. "How did Fischer's Tower get its name, Dad?" I asked. "Did the water from the lake come up to the tower so people could fish there?"

Dad laughed. "No, it has nothing to do with fishing. Fischer is spelled F-i-s-c-h-e-r. The tower is actually an old volcanic plug, the remains of a volcanic eruption years ago. Back in the late 1800s European explorers hiked through East and Central Africa, claiming bits of land for their countries, and forgot that people already lived here. The Germans controlled Tanzania. Great Britain had Zanzibar and was working on getting the area of Kenya and Uganda. So there was a race on to see who could get to Uganda first and claim that whole territory.

"At the time, the Maasai warriors who lived around here were very fierce and no caravans could make it through. A German explorer named Fischer fought his way up as far as the volcanic tower before he was pushed back by the Maasai and abandoned his trip. Fischer's Tower marks the end of the German advance."

At Hell's Gate we looked in awe at the chiseled cliffs that formed the gorge. Right in the middle was Fischer's tower, looking like a Flintstone version of the Leaning Tower of Pisa. We got out and helped Mr. Jenkins unload his ropes. He gave us a few tips, one being that we should always have three hands or feet securely gripped before reaching for a handhold or stepping for a foothold.

I watched as he took a rope and draped it over his shoulder before climbing over the jumbled piles of rock. Soon he stood at the top. He tied one end of the rope to a rock and threw it down. I tied on the waist harness like he'd shown me and we attached the rope. My dad held the bottom end.

"Follow the path I climbed," Mr. Jenkins shouted down. *Path?* I thought to myself. *What path? This is all rock!*

I headed up. It was not too hard at first. The rocks weren't too steep and there were lots of cracks to slip my feet into and to hold onto with my fingers.

Then it got steeper. I slowed down. I could see a ledge ahead. If I could reach that, the rest looked easy. But the rock in front of me bulged out like the stomach of a fat rugby player I'd seen in Nairobi playing for the Harlequins rugby team. I pushed my feet into a crack and reached as far as I could with my right hand. I couldn't quite reach the small handhold. I stretched again. Then my right foot slipped!

chapter six

MATATU
CONDUCTOR

I stabbed frantically with my right foot trying to get a grip on something. The rubber toe of my tennis shoe found nothing. I flattened my cheek against the rock and hung there with only my left arm and left foot. I couldn't hold on much longer, and my shoulder was beginning to cramp. I continued to scrabble with my right foot and hand, but couldn't get a grip. I made one last frantic attempt to pull myself back, but I didn't have the strength. My left hand slipped out of the hold and I fell backwards.

My worst nightmare flashed through my mind. It was the one where I climbed up some steep place and then slipped. But this wasn't a dream. I screamed as I fell. Then the rope caught me and I dangled back and forth.

"Are you okay?" Mr. Jenkins called, as he scrambled down from the top. Aside from the jolt I hadn't been hurt.

"I...I'm okay," I said. "Just scared. What do I do next?"

"We'll get you back to the rock face," he said. "Then I'll show you how to climb around that bulge."

"I want to go back down," I said.

"The best way down is to go up to the top," he said.

"Is everything all right up there?" my dad yelled from the bottom where he held the rope tightly. Mr. Jenkins gave him the thumbs-up. Then he reached down to stop the rope from swinging and pulled me gently to the rock where I'd slipped. "Put your toe in there," he commanded. "And your other foot there." I followed his instructions. He got my left hand back into the same grip as before. "Now, there's one handhold you can't see. You actually reached past it the first time so I know you can stretch that far. Your hand was just an inch too low."

"Kind of like when I try to reach out and shut the door to my room when it's dark," I said, trying to take my mind off my left shoulder as it began to cramp again.

"Right," he said. "You're reaching blind. But I'll guide you with my voice. Now reach out a bit farther. That's good. Now up just a bit. There, you've got it."

My right hand dug into the small crack. I leaned against the rock, spread out like an octopus trying to open up a big clam shell.

"Now it's time to move your feet," Mr. Jenkins said. "Your left foot is in a pretty good-sized crack. So move it along to your right." I did. "Now you're going to have to take a big step with your right leg. You can't see where you're going to put your foot, but I can. Is your left leg secure?"

"Yes," I said.

"Okay, put all your weight on it and push off. Be sure to keep your handholds tight."

I obeyed. "Now reach with your right leg." I couldn't feel anyplace to put my foot. But Mr. Jenkins encouraged me. "Almost there, just a bit farther." My toe found the crack and I wedged my shoe in. "Bring your left leg across to where your right foot used to be. Then you should be able to put your left hand over the top of the ledge and join me up here."

I did as he said and slowly pulled myself up onto the ledge. Mr. Jenkins smiled. "Well done. From here it's an easy climb." And it was. Within a few minutes I stood at the top and looked down.

"I made it!" I called down to the rest who clapped and cheered. But looking down made me feel sick. We were pretty high! How would we get down?

After a few minutes to catch my breath and enjoy the scenery, I posed for a picture. My dad took one from the bottom and Mr. Jenkins used a pocket camera to take one from the top.

"How will we get down?" I asked.

"We'll rappel," Mr. Jenkins said, beginning to arrange the ropes. Once he had me securely tied in the harness, he told me to hold onto the rope and walk off the top backwards, keeping my feet towards the rocks. I could go down faster or slower, depending on how I held the rope. I looked down at the jagged rocks below.

"Isn't there some other way down?" I asked.

"This is it," he said. "Don't worry, we won't let you fall."

Holding tightly to the rope I took a deep breath and stepped off the cliff backwards. I didn't let the rope run too fast. "Lean back farther," Mr. Jenkins called. I did and the rope held me in a comfortable position at a right angle to the rock face. Then I walked down the cliff, dropping steadily until I reached the bottom.

My dad reached out and set me on the ground. "Well, Dean, you did it," he said proudly.

He took off my harness and Mr. Jenkins pulled it back up. Then Mr. Jenkins rappeled down, the rope whizzing as he dropped like a spider down its web.

"You did well, Dean," he said. "Now, any of you other boys want to learn to climb?"

"I want to climb Fischer's Tower," said Matt.

"Not today," Mr. Jenkins said smiling. "That was Dean's special task. But let's drive over to some of those cliffs over there and I'll show you some climbing techniques."

We threw the gear into the Land Rover. As I sat down I noticed my hands were trembling. I folded my arms and pressed my hands to my chest. I'd been scared. Really scared. But I'd done it. I breathed a prayer of thanks to God.

At the cliffs a number of climbs had been mapped out with white paint by a rock climber's club. Mr. Jenkins took us to one that looked like a chimney. Matt and Jon climbed up easily. Dave followed in his turn, moving slowly up the rock like a gecko lizard.

Later, on a rock that only stood about ten feet off the ground, Mr. Jenkins showed us how to climb out from under an overhang. We all tried it, but only Matt and Jon had the strength to pull themselves up.

We drove home that night a happy bunch. I was especially glad I could check that task off my list. Dad kept going on about the pictures he'd taken.

When the pictures came back a few days later, I was

stunned. He'd taken the pictures looking straight up Fischer's Tower. I could see my body clinging to the sheer rock face. It made what I'd done look dangerous. I guess it was.

"I've arranged your trip to the Njoroge farm for the first week of vacation," Dad said after we'd admired the pictures. Our school had three one-month-long vacations every year so that kids who lived in the dorm didn't have to be away from their parents for too long.

The day after school got out Dad drove me up to the Njoroge's farm at a place called Solai. The farmhouse was built of wooden boards with the outer bark still on. A shiny *mabati* roof (corrugated metal sheets) covered the home with drains on the edge to catch the rainwater and funnel it into a large water tank by the side of the house. The house was surrounded by small cultivated fields. We drank *chai* with the family before Dad headed for home.

I really enjoyed the next few days. Mrs. Njoroge didn't speak much English and she had decided she would teach me to speak Kikuyu. In three days! She was a large woman and every time I said something right in Kikuyu, she'd smother me with a hug.

The first day Mr. Njoroge strapped a backpack sprayer onto my back. I held the nozzle in one hand and could pump pressure with a lever by my waist. They wanted me to spray their tomatoes, a cash crop they had just started growing. The plants had started well, but without a good dose of insecticide, the hungry bugs of Kenya would eat the tomatoes before they could be harvested. I walked up and down the rows in the scorching sun, spraying each plant.

Mrs. Njoroge cheered me on in Kikuyu. "*Ni wega*," she kept repeating. "It is good."

That evening she taught me how to milk the family cow. My fingers fumbled as I tried to tug on the cow's udder. Mrs. Njoroge laughed and squatted on the small stool. She gently pulled and the milk sprayed out like a powerful squirt gun. She let me try again and I did better the second time.

The next day Mr. Njoroge asked me to spend the day with him as the turn-boy on his *matatu*, a kind of taxi. That meant collecting money from the passengers. The white *matatu* had bright green and yellow stripes painted on it and a sign that read: Solai Tours, God is Able. After an early morning breakfast of tea, bread, and bananas, I drove with Mr. Njoroge to a crossroads where he would pick up his first passengers. The sun had just peeked over the hills. As we waited in the cool morning air, Mr. Njoroge handed me a small hand broom. I swept out the passenger area, a boxy canopy that had been built over the back of the pickup. Three black vinyl-covered benches placed lengthwise filled most of the space.

An older lady arrived with her son who carried a large gunnysack full of maize, hard corn kernels that would be taken to a mill and ground into cornmeal. Mr. Njoroge helped them throw the sack onto the roof rack. He didn't bother to tie it down. The weight of the maize would keep it from bouncing off. Mr. Njoroge told her the fare to town would be ten shillings plus five shillings for the gunnysack. She paid and climbed into the *matatu*. Mr. Njoroge showed me how to fold the ten-shilling note lengthwise and then weave it between my three middle fingers. The five-shilling coin went in my pocket.

Mr. Njoroge explained how holding it this way would keep the money handy to make change for passengers. A man climbed on. I took his twenty-shilling note, folded it as I'd been shown and put it in my hand. Then I gave him his change.

Mr. Njoroge showed me how to stand on the back step of the *matatu* hanging on to the ladder so I could hop off and hold the door open for any new passengers. Then he honked the horn twice and set off down the dirt road, avoiding holes and rocks. Dust swirled up behind us, almost choking me. We picked up more and more passengers until we had twenty people crammed into the back. It was only licensed to carry sixteen. Several people stood between the benches and crouched against the sitting passengers.

Suddenly the passengers began motioning for me to get inside. "Get in! Get in!" they cried desperately.

I pushed myself into the crowd of bodies. A young man slammed the door shut. "What's wrong?" I asked.

"Police," they said as we drove by two khaki-uniformed policemen. "If they see someone hanging on the back they'll know the vehicle is overloaded. So everyone must be inside." This time the police were busy talking to the driver of another overcrowded *matatu* so they didn't stop us.

We drove on to a large dirt area near the railroad station. Hundreds of *matatus* blared their horns as they swarmed into the area. After unloading our passengers, Mr. Njoroge parked in the jumbled confusion of vehicles. "We have a few hours until we can start collecting passengers for the ride back," he said. "We drivers have agreed to go in order. We are number seven today."

I looked at all the cars. Some had turn-boys calling out for various other destinations. I noticed a number of the turn-boys chewing on green sticks.

"What are they chewing?" I asked.

"*Miraa*," Mr. Njoroge said in disgust. "The young men think it makes them brave and fashionable. It's a twig from trees that grow near Meru. It keeps a lot of sleepy men awake and makes a lot of the turn-boys very pushy. Many of them are giving honest *matatu* drivers like me a bad name."

I nodded. "How do you know when it's your turn to collect passengers?" I asked.

Mr. Njoroge smiled. "I'll know. We all work together. Everyone going to Solai will go into that *matatu* over there. When it's full, it will leave and the number two driver will start calling for passengers. Come, let's go. I have a bad tire and I want to see about buying a new one."

The new tire cost too much. Mr. Njoroge argued over the price but finally left, shaking his head. "Tires cost so much and they wear out so quickly." We went instead to find a used tire that had been given new tread. Mr. Njoroge checked the casings of the tires on display until he found one he liked and he bought it for half the price of a new tire.

Then we went back to collect passengers. One man who got in could hardly walk. His eyes kept fluttering. He slumped into his seat and immediately fell asleep.

About half way home one of the passengers tapped on the window and Mr. Njoroge stopped the vehicle. The man who had tapped on the window then took the one I had thought was sleeping and pushed him out the door where he lay very still by the side of the road.

chapter seven

THE LEOPARD

No one went to help the man. He looked like a log by the side of the road. The *matatu* started off. "Is that man all right?" I asked a passenger who had told me he was a school teacher. The teacher wore black-framed glasses, the corner of one side taped together with white sticky tape. "I mean, he looked...dead!"

"No, he's not dead," the school teacher said sadly. "Just very drunk on a locally brewed beer called *chang'aa*. That man used to be a bright pupil in one of my classes. But when he failed to get a place in university, he became discouraged and started drinking. It's illegal, but around every town in Kenya there are places that sell it. *Chang'aa* is eating up the brains of my people. That man by the side of the road isn't dead. But he might as well be."

The school teacher got off at the stop next to the secondary school. A few stops later a young man got on with a sack of potatoes. I told him the potatoes would cost five shillings and he refused to pay. I didn't know what to do so I walked around to the driver's window and told Mr. Njoroge. He got out and the two men began to discuss the problem. Mr. Njoroge looked at me. "This man doesn't think he should have to pay the full five shillings for his potatoes since he's not traveling all the way from Nakuru. But if I carry his load for free then everyone else will want their loads carried for free." They finally settled on two shillings for the potatoes and we bumped down the road again. A chicken raced in front of the *matatu* before dodging, clucking noisily, into the grass by the roadside.

By evening I was tired. At the Njoroge's home we had a big meal and then, to my surprise, they pulled off a white cloth, embroidered with Bible verses, that hung over a black-and-white TV set. Powered by a car battery, the TV picked up the Kenya Broadcasting Corporation (KBC) very well. "Do you like football?" Mr. Njoroge asked.

I said I did. Of course I knew he meant soccer, not American football. We sat and watched two teams from the Italian League. I was in the middle of Africa at a small farm with no electricity, yet I was watching some of the best soccer in the world.

The next day was Sunday and we walked to the nearby church for the service. We sat on narrow wooden benches. It was hot in the mud-brick building. A few of the wooden window shutters had been opened to let a slight breeze pass through. The church had a number of choirs who sang before the pastor preached. There was the youth choir, the women's choir, the church choir and two sisters who sang a special number. The preacher spoke in Kikuyu and Mr. Njoroge kept up a whispered translation into my ear.

After church I stood around shaking hands with everyone. Mrs. Njoroge had left a bit early. My parents were coming to pick me up that afternoon and she wanted to feed them well.

When my parents arrived I couldn't believe what I saw. They'd brought all the Rhinos with them. "Hey, how've you been, Dean?" Matt asked, jumping out of the back of the Land Rover.

"Great," I said. "I got to be the turn-boy on a *matatu* yesterday."

Mr. Njoroge took us on a short tour of his farm, showing us the corn, tomatoes and coffee trees. He explained how he picked the red coffee berries.

When the food was ready we all sat on wooden chairs placed around the edge of the sitting room. A wooden table in the middle of the room sagged under the weight of six or seven white enamel-painted metal bowls. One contained a mound of green *irio*, a traditional Kikuyu mixture of mashed potatoes, beans, corn, and pumpkin leaves. In fact, Mrs. Njoroge had taught me that *irio* meant food in Kikuyu. Other bowls held cooked carrots, cooked cabbage, kale, arrowroot, *ugali*, a thick corn meal porridge, and small chunks of meat in gravy. A large plate was piled high with *chapatis*, thick, flat fried bread. After Mr. Njoroge thanked the Lord for the meal and guests to share it with, his wife served the food into deep plates with a half-inch lip. The lip helped hold the gravy in as it was poured over all the rest of the food. Instead of forks, we each took several *chapatis* and used them to shovel in our meals. It was excellent.

After the gigantic meal we drank *chai* and burped softly. Then Mr. Njoroge asked my dad to lead everyone in a short devotional. We sang some Kikuyu songs and then Dad spoke from Ephesians. After some prayer time, we got up to leave. Of course the Njoroge family kept protesting and asking us to stay. But Dad said he wanted to have time to stop by the Nakuru Game Park on the way home. He'd seen the pink fringe of the lake on his way to Solai that morning. He knew the lake was full of flamingos and he wanted to take some pictures.

I thanked Mr. and Mrs. Njoroge for taking the time to teach me how they lived. Then we piled into the car and drove back toward Nakuru. From there we followed the signs down to the entrance to Lake Nakuru, a shallow lake.

After paying our park fees at the gate, we drove down through the acacia forest, past majestic waterbuck with wide, heavy horns. We parked the car on the edge of the lake. "Just look at all those flamingos," Dad said, taking his camera and walking on the ashy mud at the lakeshore. Then he knelt down to get a better angle for his pictures.

We walked around on the shore for awhile collecting beautiful pink feathers. My little brother Craig grabbed handfuls of feathers, shouting with delight every time he saw another one. After Dad had enough pictures, he suggested driving around the far side of the lake to see what other animals we could find. We saw crowds of wart hogs and interrupted one with a thick black mane as he dug grubs from under an old log. Seeing us, the wart hog jerked to his feet and trotted away, his pencil-thick tail sticking straight up in the air.

We laughed and drove on. We saw giraffes, two reedbuck, and even a few cape buffalo. As we drove around one corner my dad saw a herd of orange-pelted impala with their graceful horns. "Their orange skins and the light of the sun would make a beautiful picture," Dad murmured as he stopped and fumbled to get his camera ready.

My little brother Craig, in the middle front seat over the gear shift, had been looking out the other window. "Yeah," he agreed. "I never knew impala had such beautiful spots."

"Impala don't have spots," Dad began. We all turned to look. There on our left crouched a leopard, half hidden behind a bush. We'd parked our car right between a leopard and the herd of impala!

"Close your windows," Dad said. As we did, the leopard, realizing he'd been seen, melted into the shadows.

"Looks like we disturbed his hunting," Dad said. "Did you see the way that leopard was eyeing those impala?"

"I liked the way the leopard's muscles rippled as he turned," Jon said.

"I've never seen a leopard before," Dave said.

"They're pretty hard to see," my dad said. "They usually hunt at night. Then they spend their days sleeping up in trees. About the best way to see them is to look for their striped tail dangling down from a tree. A leopard does a good job of hiding, but they always seem to forget to tuck up their tail."

He turned to Craig. "And you saw the leopard first, Craig. You're really good at finding animals."

Craig grinned. "I wondered why you said you were looking at impalas when I saw that animal with spots."

"We'd better head for home," Dad said and we turned and drove out of the park. Some zebras scattered off the road as we came near the gate.

That night I asked my dad if I could start running my thirty miles. "I know there's not quite thirty days left of vacation, but maybe on some days I could run two miles. At school we'll have a rugby team for fourth through sixth graders this year. I've never played rugby before. But I know I need to get in shape."

"This would be a good time to get started," Dad agreed. "Do you want to go tomorrow? I could run with you in the morning. I have a trail I use through the forest that's about a mile and a half. If we ran the trail once a day you'd finish your thirty miles in about twenty days."

The next morning I got up at 6:30 A.M. with my dad. He led me down the trail below our house. The forest was full of the sounds of birds and monkeys. The first part of the trail was fairly flat. Then we came to a part Dad simply called the hill. It was a steep section that led up the side of a ravine to an old back road into Rugendo. About half way up the hill, I had to stop.

"Dad, I can't go on," I gasped. "My lungs are on fire."

He stopped with me. "Just take a minute to rest," he said, barely panting himself. "Each day you'll build your endurance a bit more. This hill climbing will build your legs for rugby better than any other exercise in the world."

The heaving of my chest slowed down. I looked at my dad and nodded. "I'm all right now. Let's go."

We continued our climb up the hill to the old road. Then

we followed the old road back around to Rugendo and down to our house. The whole run had taken twenty minutes. "As you get fitter you'll be able to run it faster," Dad said, leading the way into the kitchen. He grabbed some green Kikuyu bananas and put them on the table. As I peeled one to eat, Dad took down his worn brown Bible. "This is the time I usually read my Bible," he said.

"Go ahead," I said between bites into the banana. "I won't bother you." Then I went to my room.

If Dad reads his Bible now, maybe I should read mine as well, I thought, and laid down on my bed. I found my place in the book of Isaiah which was part of my reading list for my twelve tasks. I liked the way I felt after the exercise and the reading, like my body and my mind were ready to face the day.

I kept running with my dad every morning. Soon I no longer had to stop halfway up the hill and that cut our time down to fifteen minutes. Then one morning when I got up, he hadn't gotten out of bed yet. I sneaked into my parents' room. Dad groaned and turned over. "Are you going to run today, Dad?" I asked.

"No," he said. "I was on patrol last night and we stayed up extra late chasing off some guys someone saw lurking around the station. Go ahead and run on your own."

I did. I enjoyed the clean, fresh smell of the forest in the early morning. But without my dad the forest seemed to be darker, scarier than usual. A bushbuck barked and crashed through the bushes as I ran, scaring me. As I came to the hill I ran hard, trying to get out of the forest and onto the road. But the steep hill slowed me down. And about halfway up the hill I noticed some half-chewed greenish twigs near the base of a wild olive tree.

I stopped to see what it was.

chapter eight

THE
RUGBY GAME

I knelt by the partly-chewed twigs and recognized them. "It's that *miraa* stuff I saw the turn-boys chewing in Nakuru," I said out loud even though no one was with me. "I wonder if this has something to do with the group of men my dad saw last night?"

I continued my climb up the hill and jogged home. I tried to tell my dad about the *miraa* I'd seen but he was too tired to respond. "Later, Dean, later," he yawned and turned over tucking a pillow over his head.

There's probably no connection, I thought. But that morning at our tree house I told the other Rhinos what I'd seen. Matt, presiding over our club meeting, scratched his head as he thought about it.

"So you think maybe the people who have been breaking in around the station are using *miraa*," Matt said. "It sounds reasonable if *miraa* works on people like you said it does, making them feel real tough and unbeatable. Anyway, let's go see this *miraa*."

We climbed down from the tree house. "You lead the way, Dean," Matt said. I rarely led on our hikes, but I started off jogging through the forest. Soon the others called for me to slow down.

"We haven't been running every morning like you have," Dave panted as the others caught up.

When we got to the place on the hill where I'd seen the *miraa*, I stopped and pointed to the chewed green twigs.

"How does the drug work?" Matt asked.

"I'm not sure," I said. "I just know it has to be chewed. Somehow it makes *miraa* chewers very jumpy, loud and obnoxious. And it keeps chewers from falling asleep. A lot of truck drivers chew it to stay awake on the road. At least that's what I'm told."

"Chew it, huh?" Matt asked. "I wonder what it tastes like?"

"Matt, you can't chew that stuff!" I protested. "Besides being a drug, those sticks have already been chewed."

"Yeah," Jon said, scrumpling up his nose in disgust, "that's even worse than ABC gum."

ABC gum was Jon's trick that he played on all new kids coming to our school. He would offer them some ABC gum. The kids, thinking it was some kind of Kenyan brand, would ask for a piece. They'd be grossed out as Jon removed a wad of gum from his mouth and started to give it to them. "ABC gum," he'd say. "Already Been Chewed."

"I wouldn't really try any," Matt said. He kicked the sticks with his foot. "Well, if any of you guys see anyone around Rugendo chewing *miraa*, maybe that will give us a clue as to who's behind the break-ins. The police sure haven't caught anyone. And all our dads seem to be able to do is keep them away with all their patrolling."

But we never caught another hint of *miraa* use around the station.

Vacation ended about the same time I finished running my thirty miles. I felt fit and strong the first day of school when one of the teachers announced tryouts for the Titchie Colts rugby team. A colt team was a British rugby term for a junior team where younger players learned how to play the game of rugby. Our school had a First Fifteen and a Second Fifteen, kind of like a varsity and junior varsity in the States. Then there were the colts teams. There was Senior Colts, Middle Colts, Junior Colts, and now a new team, Titchie Colts.

All of us Rhinos went to the tryouts. As we stood on the grassy field, we listened to the coach explaining the game of rugby. All we knew was that you could carry the ball and you had to pass it backwards. And you could tackle anyone with the ball. It looked cool when we saw the big kids in school playing. I wasn't sure I really wanted to tackle someone though. What if I got my head banged around by the runner's knees?

The first practice the coach taught us how to pass a rugby ball with two hands. We did several drills running up and down the field. Then we ran and did push-ups. I stayed ahead on the running. My push-ups, though, were kind of weak. If I bent my elbows, my arms collapsed and I landed on my chest in the grass. I bobbed my head up and down without moving my elbows. The coach never saw my pitiful attempts. Matt and Jon did real push-ups, their wiry arms flexing like a python squeezing its prey.

"You all did well for a first practice," the coach said. "Tomorrow afternoon I'll teach you how to tackle without getting hurt. And then I'll teach you how to form down for a scrum and how to set up a line-out. After a few days we'll start to scrimmage so you can see how the game goes."

"I can't wait until we can tackle!" Jon said as we walked home after practice.

"That will be great!" Matt agreed. "Smearing people into the ground."

I felt scared to death of tackling. But I wasn't about to admit it in front of the other Rhinos.

I didn't enjoy the next day of school. The thought of tackling practice filled my mind. I had almost decided to go home saying I felt sick. But I knew I couldn't pretend to be sick all term. So I went.

"Now to teach you how to tackle properly," our coach said, "I want you first to find a partner."

Jon and Matt paired up. I looked at Dave and he nodded.

"Now get on your knees," the coach said. Then from a kneeling position, the coach showed us how to wrap our arms completely around the runner's legs. "If you do it this way, you won't get hurt," the coach said. "Your head and neck will be safely to the side. Your shoulder will hit the softest part of the leg. Your arms will tie the runner's legs together. With his legs slammed together by your tackle, his own weight and forward momentum will knock him over. And you'll land on top of him."

What he said made sense and it encouraged me. And doing it on our knees was a fairly painless way of learning to tackle. Except for our knees themselves. The grass was prickly and in spots there was no grass at all, only red dirt.

After everyone had learned the basics of tackling, the coach encouraged us to turn it into a game. Still on our knees, the runner now tried to avoid the tackler. And then it was time to try it standing up. The first time I did it, Dave was only trotting slowly. But it still scared me. I closed my eyes as I reached out to tackle him. To my surprise, Dave fell over and I landed on top of him. Just like it was supposed to happen. Then Dave tackled me. By the end of the practice I'd gotten over my basic fear. It wasn't my favorite part of rugby, but at least I wasn't scared to death.

As the coach began to assemble the team for our first scrimmage, he put me in as a lock forward together with Dave. He showed us how to bind onto each other tightly and then insert our heads between the hips of the front row forwards. "Ow, that hurts," I said as my ears were shoved roughly between the front row players. The coach looked down at me. "It hurts at first," he said. "But you'll get used to it."

"Something's scratching me," Dave said. The coach looked. The prop forward on his side was wearing a pair of cut-off jeans. The rivets on the corners of the pockets were raking the side of Dave's head. "Now that won't do," the coach said. "No more cut-off jeans for playing rugby," he announced, and then pulled in another boy who had shorts with no metal parts.

The first time we put the ball in the scrum, the whole thing collapsed on top of Dave and me. Matt and Jon, who had been assigned to play fullback and wing and didn't have to be in the middle of the scrum, started laughing at us. The coach warned them that he'd stick them in the next scrum if they made fun of us. Then he unpiled us and helped us do it again. After half an hour of practice my ears had small cuts under the ear lobes. But our scrum was doing better. We had learned how to push and to hook the ball back to our players so they could run with it.

We began scrimmaging the next day. It seemed like total confusion at first, but gradually we learned how to get behind the backs and support them when they were tackled.

"You're looking pretty good," our coach said. "Now, our first game is next Wednesday against a British school in Nairobi called Sterling Academy." We all cheered. "There's a lot more to learn," he said, "but now you'll have to learn it by playing against some good opposition."

That next Wednesday we strutted around class all afternoon in our uniforms. We had been allowed to change at lunch since the bus left right after school. My soccer cleats clattered as I walked on the gray tile floor of the classroom. "Good luck," Jill whispered to me.

"Thanks," I mumbled, feeling my face get hot. I wondered if she liked me. She hadn't said much to me since we'd been joint winners of the creativity award in the Pinewood Derby.

As we got on the bus, the butterflies in my stomach began to flutter. It was our first rugby game. I sat with Dave, Jon, and Matt. The others talked nonstop about how good they would play. I just prayed I wouldn't make any big mistakes.

On the way to Nairobi it started to rain. "The only way to play rugby, boys," our coach said turning around. "In the mud."

The field at Sterling Academy looked like a swamp. Puddles covered the field and rain still poured down. "Won't they cancel the game?" I asked the coach.

"Not for a rugby game," he said, smiling and unfurling his big black umbrella. "Now use the bathrooms and then let's get down on the field."

After a few reminders from our coach, the ref blew his whistle for the coin toss. Matt went out as our captain for the day. We lost the coin toss and Sterling decided to kick off to us. As we stood back to receive the kickoff, I felt like a whole herd of butterflies had been unleashed in my stomach.

Sterling kicked off. The oval ball floated end over end. It was coming straight for me! I called for it, tried to catch it, but in the wet rain the leather ball was slick and I knocked it forward. The ref blew his whistle. We had to have a scrum. Gritting my teeth I bound together with Dave and we got set for the scrum. We didn't collapse, but the Sterling forwards drove us back. Their scrum half picked up the ball and passed it out to his waiting backs. They had a big redheaded boy at first center. He crashed right through the middle. None of our players wanted to tackle him. Even Matt looked scared and only tried to push the redhead over. It didn't work. The redhead ran over the line and set the ball down right between the posts. Sterling had scored. They kicked the conversion and Sterling led 7-0.

Our coach pleaded from the sidelines. "Tackle like I taught you, boys. Don't be afraid. The bigger they are, the harder they fall."

"Easy for him to say," Matt said, annoyed.

The game got worse. We kicked off to the Sterling

forwards who ran the ball straight back at us. We parted like the Red Sea and they scored again.

"Come on, Dean," Matt complained. "You moved out of that guy's way."

I didn't say anything, but I'd noticed Matt didn't come across to make the tackle like a fullback is supposed to do. On this kickoff I determined not to move out of the way. As a burly Sterling player caught the ball and started running, I crouched down and then aimed my shoulder and tackled him, just like we'd been taught. The player went down with a splash in a puddle. "Good job, Dean," Dave said. But while we congratulated ourselves on making a tackle, the Sterling forwards took over the ball again.

This time the redheaded center ran straight at Matt. But now Matt dug his shoulder in and tackled the redhead. They both crashed into the mud and slid along the ground. The redhead dropped the ball and it rolled forward. The ref blew his whistle. The redhead got up as we gathered for the scrum, but Matt just lay on the ground, not moving.

chapter nine

THE RESTAURANT

"Matt! Matt! Are you okay?" I asked, kneeling beside him.

Matt gave a low moan. The ref came over as our team crowded around. "Give him air, boys, give him air. He'll be fine."

Matt gulped in a big breath and his eyes opened. Then he started breathing more regularly.

"Just got the wind knocked out of him," the ref announced, giving Matt a hand. Matt stood up and took a few more gulps of air. "Can you play?" the ref asked. Matt nodded. The ref blew his whistle for the game to go on.

We did a little better. Matt began tackling hard, like he'd had the fear knocked out of him along with the wind. But we didn't have the teamwork and support that Sterling did. They scored several more goals and led by over thirty points at halftime.

The rain stopped in the second half, but the field was slipperier than ever. Steam rose from the field as the sun beamed down on the marshy grass. We gave up a few more scores and even had a few chances to run with the ball. I leaped high and caught the ball. I tossed it to the scrum half and our backs passed the ball without dropping it. They got it to Jon who tucked the ball under his arm and ran like a cheetah. It had been his first chance all game to run with the ball. He got tackled out of bounds after making about ten yards. We all cheered his run.

But with only a few minutes left we were losing 54-0. Then the Sterling forwards were caught offside. We had a penalty kick. "I can make it," Matt said. He spoke to the ref. "We'd like to go for poles, sir." The ref signaled that we would be taking a kick on goal. Matt set the ball up in a scuff mark that he made with his heel. Then he stepped back four large steps. He looked at the goal post which was almost identical to the goal post on an American football field. Then he looked at the ball. Taking a deep breath he ran, swung, and stroked the ball perfectly with his right foot. Then he slipped in the mud and landed on his rear end. But the ball flew straight at the goal post. It hit the crossbar and bounced over. The kick was good! We'd scored three points! The ref blew his whistle three times to signal the end of the game. We had lost 54-3.

Mud-stained, we gave three cheers to the winners and then ran through the tunnel the Sterling team formed at the end of the field. They shook our hands as we walked through and then invited us to join them for refreshments. We sat around drinking orange juice and eating cookies, or biscuits as the Sterling players had called them.

Our coach walked around and shook hands with each of us. "You worked hard," he complimented me. "You've learned what real rugby is all about."

Even though we'd lost we felt like we'd won a victory of sorts by at least scoring. And we had overcome that uncontrollable fear of tackling a big player running straight at you. On the bus on the way home we sang songs we'd heard the older players at school singing after rugby games. One was a Zulu song from South Africa.

Izaaka zimba zimba zimba,
Izaaka zimba zimba zee,
Izaaka zimba zimba zimba,
Izaaka zimba zimba zee,
Hold him down you Zulu warrior
Hold him down you Zulu chief.

Then half the team chanted, "Chief, chief, chief," while the other half of the team repeated the verse.

We were a hyper group of boys by the time the bus neared Rugendo. As we slowed down for some sharp curves on the steep road that snaked into the mission station, I looked out the window. I saw six or seven Kenyan boys walking by the side of the road. It was just getting dark so I couldn't see very well. But the boys had an angry glare in their eyes. I saw one of them shaking a fist at our bus.

Then I saw a larger person wearing a navy-blue knitted wool ski hat. He raised his arm to cover his face and then turned to hide behind a tree. As he turned I thought I saw a stick of *miraa* jutting from his mouth. "Look, Dave," I said. "It looks like that guy's chewing *miraa!*"

Dave tried to look out the window. "I don't see anything, Dean. Are you sure? It's getting dark." We could see the orange glow of the end of a cigarette that one of the boys was puffing on. "Are you sure you didn't see a cigarette?"

"Maybe," I admitted. "But it wasn't glowing. Oh, I don't know. It was pretty dark and I'm looking for *miraa* everywhere to prove my theory."

As we drove onto the school compound we asked the bus driver to honk the horn. He refused politely saying the tradition was to honk the horn when a team won. "Don't worry," he laughed. "You'll have plenty of chances to roar into school with the horn blowing as you grow older and start winning games."

We ate shepherd's pie in the school cafeteria. We Rhinos sat at a table together. Matt, who was jealous of the hair on my legs, took hold of one of the red clots of hardened mud now clinging to my leg hairs and asked, "Odds or evens?"

Before I could answer he gave a yank, ripping a strip of hairs off my leg. "Ouch!" I cried. "Matt, knock it off!"

The coach, supervising the meal, raised his eyebrows at us from another table. Matt dropped his voice. "Come on, Dean. Guess. Odds or evens. We'll count the hairs I pulled out. Did I pull out an odd number or an even number? If you guess right I'll buy you a Coke."

"Evens," I said grumpily and went on eating while Matt counted out the hairs.

"Sixteen," Matt said. "You were right, Dean. It was evens. Come on, let's do it again. Double or nothing."

I pulled my leg away. "Only if we do it on your leg," I said.

"I don't think so," Matt replied. "It's a stupid game, anyway."

We finished eating and scraped off our trays and stacked them in the dishwashing room.

At home I told my parents about the game. Dad listened, fascinated. Mom told me I needed to take a bath.

After my bath we had our family devotions. When we'd finished reading the Bible and praying, Mom asked when I wanted to create my own restaurant and cook a meal for four guests.

"I don't know," I said. "I really hadn't thought much about that task."

"I was thinking you could do it this Friday night," Mom said. "It's the Freedmans' wedding anniversary—"

"Hey, our anniversary is on Saturday," Dad said.

I looked at Mom. "So you thought I could have the Freedmans and you two come to my restaurant?"

"Sounds like a cheap date," Dad said.

"You haven't seen the prices at my restaurant," I answered.

Dad laughed.

"Why don't you decide on your menu now," Mom said. "I'm going to Nairobi tomorrow and I can buy the food you need."

"Can I get the other Rhinos to help me?" I asked. "A restaurant will need chefs and waiters and things like that."

"Sure they can help," she said. Then she grabbed a tablet and asked what I wanted to serve.

"Meat," I answered. "We have to serve meat."

"Of course, but what kind?"

"I hate liver," I said.

"But, Dean, you're not the one eating," Mom reminded me.

I nodded. "True, but if the look of liver makes the cook gag, then he's not going to do a very good job of cooking it."

"What about chicken?" my mom asked.

"Sure, I could bake some chicken with that Italian sauce you make."

My mom nodded and jotted down chicken on her list. "The sauce is easy to make," she said. "And I have all the spices you'll need. Now what about a salad?"

We agreed on a tossed salad, French bread, the chicken, and baked potatoes. That way I could cook the chicken and potatoes in the oven while I made the salad.

"And what will you make for dessert?" Mom asked.

I thought. "Couldn't you buy a half-gallon of Dairyland ice cream? Then we could eat what was left over."

"Ice cream is good," Mom said slowly, "but you might want to make it into something fancier. Maybe I could buy some strawberries and you could learn from Dad how to make those thin Swedish pancakes. Then you could put ice cream and strawberries inside and call it crêpes suzette or something fancy like that."

"Okay," I said, "as long as the cooks get to eat the leftovers."

The next day at school I asked the other Rhinos to help me with the restaurant. They weren't too interested until they found out we could eat the extras. That evening I made four menus for my restaurant, which I called *Chakula Kizuri*, Swahili for Good Food.

I wrote down the entrees and at the bottom wrote that the complete meal would cost fifty shillings per person. I really didn't expect them to pay. But I wanted my restaurant to look official.

On Friday after school the other guys came over and we got to work in the kitchen. My mom had organized everything. We followed the recipes, making the sauce for the chicken first. Then we put the chicken and potatoes in the oven before making the salad. Dad had helped me make the Swedish pancakes the day before and they were ready to be filled with ice cream and strawberries.

I told Dave how I wanted the table to look and he laid it out precisely. We even had some candles. Dave and Jon would act as the waiters and I'd talked them into wearing button-down shirts and black neckties. Matt and I would serve the food from the kitchen.

The Freedmans arrived all dressed up and Dave and Jon escorted them to the table. My parents came out dressed in fancy clothes as well. Dave and Jon took the drink orders. We offered Coke, Fanta, or Sprite. Then they served the salad followed by the main dish. And, finally, the dessert.

After the meal was over, the adults, who had been talking quietly and enjoying their meal, turned to us in the kitchen. *"Chakula kizuri,"* my dad said. *"Ni tamu sana.* The food is good, it's very sweet."

We all smiled and bowed. Then they each took out fifty shillings to pay for the meal. That made fifty shillings for each of us.

"All right!" I said. "Our restaurant made money."

"Not quite so fast," Mom said smiling. "You have to pay for the food from the money your guests pay." She showed me her receipts. I hadn't left much of a profit margin. Maybe I wouldn't make a very good businessman.

"Why don't you move into more comfortable chairs in our lounge," I told the Freedmans and my parents, ushering them toward our living room.

"All right," I whispered to the other guys. "Now we can scarf down the food that's still in the kitchen."

Just then we heard the pig-squealing sound of an air horn.

chapter ten

HEADING FOR MT. KENYA

My dad and Dr. Freedman got up right away. "Lock the house after we leave," Dad said. "We'll find out what's going on."

They went out and drove away in the Land Rover. We couldn't really enjoy our food, wondering if someone else had been hurt in a break-in.

The men came back after about ten minutes looking annoyed. "What happened? Was anyone hurt?" Mom asked.

"It was a false alarm," Dad said. "Some of the junior high boys are having a sleep over at the Bartons' house. They decided to play a game of *posho.*"

"What's *posho?*" Matt asked. "I thought it was the Swahili word for cornmeal mush."

"It is," my dad answered. "But a few years ago the missionary kids at school got the idea of sneaking out of the dorm at night and then knocking on windows at mission houses. They hid in the bushes and had a good laugh while the missionary in the house tried to figure out what was going on. When they felt the missionary had suffered long enough, they jumped out of the bushes and shouted, 'Posho.' I guess they liked the sound of the word."

"Sounds like a great game," Matt said.

Dr. Freedman looked at him sharply. "Not now when there have been real break-ins and everyone is on edge. Mrs. Barton almost had a nervous breakdown after those kids tapped on the windows a few times."

"It wasn't a very nice prank," Dad agreed. "But at least it wasn't a real break-in."

We went back to the kitchen and cleaned up the dishes.

After we finished, Dad said he and Dr. Freedman had been talking about my climb up Mt. Kenya. "We thought all you Rhinos might like to climb together," he said. "And Dr. Freedman wants to climb, too. We thought the best time to climb would be in December just after Christmas."

"But, Dad," I protested, "that's almost six months away."

"True, but you can't climb Mt. Kenya anytime you want. Certain times of the year the climbing is closed because of bad weather on the peaks. Right now it's closed. It opens for a few months around August but it's usually bitterly cold. Remember, Mt. Kenya is over 16,000 feet high at Point Lenana where we'll be climbing. I think we'd be better off trying for December after Christmas when the weather is a little warmer."

I really didn't want to wait that long. But I didn't have much choice.

"It will also give us a chance to make reservations," Dad said. "We'll have to book bunks both at the Met Station and at Mackinder's Camp. Sometimes during climbing season all the bunks are booked. So we'd best do it early."

All the Rhinos went home with instructions to get permission from their parents to make the climb. Then my dad would make the bookings. Everyone would have to gather his own climbing gear: backpacks, gloves, coats, winter hats, climbing boots, and anything else we might need.

After the other guys had all left I asked my dad if Kamau could climb with us. My dad thought for awhile. "I think that would be okay. As long as his parents let him go. But we'll probably have to help him with the gear."

The next day I walked over to Kamau's house to ask him if he could join us in the hike up Mt. Kenya. "When is it?" Kamau asked, excited about getting a chance to climb the mountain. "My tribe says that it was on top of Mt. Kenya, which my people call *Kirinyaga*, that *Ngai*, God, placed the first man, *Gikuyu*."

"We'll be climbing the last week of December," I said.

Kamau's eager smile reversed itself into a sad frown. "In December? I can't go in December."

"Why not?" I asked.

"That's the month I get circumcised," Kamau said.

"You can't change it?"

Kamau shook his head. "There are a group of us boys being circumcised together. Some of the parents in the church felt it would be good to hold a camp where all of us boys who are ready to go through the ritual could do it together. We're going to a kind of church camp for two weeks of teaching on how to be men of God. Then we'll be circumcised at a small mission hospital. And it's all organized for December. I'm sorry, Dean. I'd really like to climb Mt. Kenya with you. But I can't. That's when I'll become a man." I was disappointed, but I understood. Now that I had twelve tasks to perform, becoming a man was important to me, too.

The months passed by quickly. My dad held a soccer camp for all of us Rhinos during our August vacation. We invited other missionary kids from the station and Kamau and some of his friends.

I also got a chance to play golf with my dad. I shot a ninety. That's because I only played nine holes and my dad wouldn't let me count past ten on any hole. But I did make a few good swings and only lost six balls.

I finished memorizing the book of Colossians. It wasn't easy but I took it a few verses at a time. I worked on it in bed at night and it helped me fall asleep.

"I'm proud of you, Dean," Mom said. "It takes hard work to memorize that much of the Bible." She gave me a big hug and I felt more grown-up already.

I read all the books on my reading list and even finished the Bible study on Daniel. The only things left on my Twelve Tasks of Manhood list were to climb Mt. Kenya and eat out at the Carnivore.

"Dad, can I eat out at the Carnivore soon?" I asked one evening. "I'm done with all the other tasks except climbing Mt. Kenya."

"I want to keep that task for last," he said. "The night before your thirteenth birthday in January."

I had now moved into sixth grade. Matt was in seventh

and we didn't see each other during the school day anymore. But we were still the Rugendo Rhinos with club meetings on Saturday mornings and hikes and hunting in the forest.

Finally the day came to climb the mountain. We would stay at the Naro Moru River Lodge, the main base for climbing Mt. Kenya. We got up early in the morning and packed everything into our Land Rover. We drove through Nairobi and stopped at the Blue Posts Hotel in Thika for a mid-morning snack of sodas and *samosas*, deep-fried triangular pastries filled with spicy meat. Soon after Thika we caught a glimpse of Mt. Kenya with its rugged peaks draped in clouds. But soon the clouds covered the mountain completely.

At Naro Moru River Lodge we stopped at the mountaineering shop. Jon and his dad hadn't been able to find gloves and planned to rent some from the shop. While Jon and his dad found some warm winter mittens, Dad bought some big plastic bags to cover our sleeping bags in case it rained.

"Look at this map," Dave said. A large contour map of Mt. Kenya had been pinned to the wall. A red line showed the Naro Moru route up through the Teleki Valley.

"And there's Point Lenana," I said, pointing to where Lenana hid behind the two bigger peaks, Nelion and Batian. All three peaks had been named for Maasai spiritual leaders from the turn of the century.

"Let's stop for a Coke," Dad said, leading us downstairs into the large lounge surrounding the hotel's bar. A sign said: No One Under Eighteen Permitted.

"I think it will be okay for you guys to go in. It's the middle of the day." The bartenders were happy for the business. As we drank our sodas we walked around the room. On one wall we saw a beautiful aerial photo of the mountain.

"What are all those T-shirts?" Matt asked. Various T-shirts had been thumbtacked along the wall at ceiling level. One had the name of a British navy ship on it and then about ten names written on it in ink. At the bottom it said: Survived Mt. Kenya, Reached Point Lenana, January 14, 1985. Other shirts were from mountaineering clubs or small groups that had climbed the mountain. Some had funny stories written on them about people getting stuck in the bog.

"Dad, if we make it to the top, can we put up a shirt for the Rugendo Rhinos?" I asked.

"We could do that," he answered. "But first, we'd better climb the mountain."

We got back in the Land Rover and drove onto the dirt road leading to Mt. Kenya National Park. We stopped at a small building owned by the Mt. Kenya Guides and Porters Club to hire a guide and some porters to help carry our gear. Dad wanted me to carry my own pack as part of my task. I'd been practicing hiking around Rugendo with a loaded pack. The others all planned to carry their own packs as well. But my dad had decided to hire two porters to carry the food. That would make each of our packs a little lighter.

Inside the office, the clerk insisted that we hire two guides instead of one. We Rhinos sat on a wooden bench as my dad and Dr. Freedman discussed whether to hire one guide or two. A red calendar hung on the wall. It showed a soccer player holding a trophy while his teammates swarmed around him. *Sportsman ni sawa hasa*, the calendar read. It meant, Sportsman is especially good. Sportsman is a Kenyan-made brand of cigarettes.

"That soccer team could never win," Matt said. "Guys who smoke can't catch their breath."

I noticed the calendar was two years out of date.

My dad finally agreed that two guides would be a good idea. If, on the final climb, one of us got sick or couldn't make it, then one guide could help that person back to camp while the others climbed on. With only one guide we'd all have to keep climbing or all turn back.

"I'm sure we'll all make it," I said.

"We'd all like to make it to the top," Dr. Freedman said. "But altitude sickness can really knock a person down."

"How?" Matt asked.

"The most common signs are headache and vomiting," he answered.

"Yuck," Matt said. "Who wants to hurl on top of the mountain?"

Dr. Freedman smiled. "I've brought medicine that helps prevent altitude sickness. I'll hand it out this evening with supper."

Outside, a group of men leaned against the building. These were the guides and porters. The clerk called out four names and the men rushed over to us. An argument broke out between the clerk and two other men. After some sharp words, the men walked away sulkily and the clerk explained. "We have a lot of men desperate to get work. There's always someone who complains that I've made a mistake. We have a strict order and each man gets his chance. But they must wait their turn."

The four men assigned to take us up the mountain asked for half an hour to collect their hiking gear. We waited. Finally one of the men, who said his name was Francis, came back. He wore a black *kabooti*, a military coat. He tossed his backpack, held together by a snarl of sisal string, into the back of the Land Rover. "I'm your lead guide for this climb," Francis said. "Let's go. We'll pick the others up on the road."

The other three were waiting a couple of miles farther up the road. "You're in luck," Francis said. "There's been no rain. Last week it rained so hard no cars could get farther than the gate to the park. That added six miles of hiking for all the climbers."

We paid our entrance fees at the gate. "Look at that poster!" Dave said. A photocopied picture of a young man's bearded face stared out at us off the worn sheet of paper. Lost, the small poster said, Wanted: information on the whereabouts of Jeremy Sloan, last seen at Mackinder's Camp planning to climb to Point Lenana. The sign gave a description and the date Sloan was reported missing.

"That was over a year ago!" I said.

The warden looked stern. "Be careful. Mt. Kenya is not hard to climb. But if you act foolishly and try to climb alone, bad things can happen."

"What do you think happened to him?" I asked Dad.

"Who knows," he answered. "He could have had a heart attack or altitude sickness. He could have walked over a cliff in the dark." He stopped. "The mountain can be a dangerous place."

I felt a chill run down my back. And it came from more than the cold late afternoon mist that had settled on the forest. Climbing Mt. Kenya might not be as easy as I thought.

chapter eleven

HIKING UP THE VERTICAL BOG

Before we left the gate, my dad, as usual, gave the wardens copies of the Christian magazine he edited. Both wardens had their heads bent over the pages before we'd gotten back into the car. We had to call out for one of them to open the big metal gate with the silhouette of a rhino in the center.

"Looks like this is our park," Matt said, joking. "The Rugendo Rhinos drive through the rhino gate."

Francis asked my dad if his crew could have some magazines to read. He handed them back. The road began to wind through some huge trees. "These are podo trees," Dad said.

"We have a few near Rugendo, but here in the high rain forest they grow to an immense size."

A few mud holes covered the road, but the Land Rover sailed right through. The last bit of the road was really steep and bumpy. We drove over a narrow wooden bridge with a sign saying it had been built by the British Army. The Land Rover slid gently in the mud before it reached a rough strip of concrete on the road that gave vehicles enough traction to climb the last hairpin bends. The concrete had big rough lines grooved into it like the ramp on a boat launch.

We finally made it up to a collection of cabins. A sign board announced that we'd arrived at the Met Station at over 10,000 feet above sea level.

"Met is short for meteorological," Dad said. "It was originally built to study the weather, take readings of rainfall, and things like that. But it became a base for climbers going up the mountain. So Naro Moru River Lodge built a bunch of smaller cabins with bunks. And that's where we're going to spend the night."

Francis and the guides said they'd meet us at 6 A.M. to start our climb. Then they went to their bunkhouse.

Dad checked in with the man in charge who then led the way to our cabin. It had ten bunks, each with a mattress. A table stood in front of a fireplace. There was a small cubicle outside with a faucet and sink. This was our cookhouse. For a bathroom, we shared an outhouse with several other cabins.

"Throw your sleeping bags on a bunk," my dad said, "and let's make our supper."

We made spaghetti. My mom had sent the sauce already made so we heated that up on one small butane gas cookstove. Then we cooked the noodles. They got pretty slimy and sticky. It took longer for them to cook because of the higher altitude. Dr. Freedman said it was because water boiled at a lower temperature. The spaghetti was stuck together in wads but it still tasted good after a long day on the road.

After supper Dr. Freedman gave each of us a clear Fuji film canister with some small white pills. "This is diamox," he said. "It will help prevent altitude sickness. You need to take one three times a day. We may get separated as we hike so I'm giving each of you your own medicine. The film canisters are waterproof." We took the pills with our *chai*, the sweet Kenyan tea that signaled the end of any meal.

Then we helped wash the dishes — a difficult task because the mountain spring water coming out of the faucet was icy cold. And my dad had forgotten to bring any dish-cloths or scouring pads. So we scraped off the spaghetti with our fingernails in the near-freezing water.

We spent a little while organizing our packs. Then we snuggled into our sleeping bags. The cold had already crept into the cabin and we didn't have any logs for the fireplace. Dad prayed for our trip and Dr. Freedman read from Psalm 124. "I lift my eyes to the hills. Where does my help come from? My help comes from the Lord." He gave a short talk on how the people who lived in Canaan before Israel had worshiped their idols in high places. But our help as believers didn't come from the hills. It came from the God who created the mountains.

After devotions my dad tuned in the British Broadcasting Corporation on his small black shortwave radio and we listened to half an hour of world news.

Then we drifted off to sleep. In the middle of the night I suddenly woke up. My bladder felt like it would explode! I fumbled my way out of the sleeping bag and stumbled down the ladder from the top bunk. On the floor I collided with Matt. "Man, something's wrong with me," Matt said. "I've got to go to the bathroom like crazy!"

We pushed open the door and found Jon already on the porch. "I have to go to the outhouse," Jon said, "but I forgot to put on any shoes and my feet are freezing." We all stood on the cement porch in our bare feet.

"I can't wait long enough to put shoes on," Matt said, and began watering the grass from where he stood on the porch. Jon and I did the same. Before we had finished Dave came out followed by Dr. Freedman and my dad.

Dr. Freedman chuckled. "I should've warned you about that medicine," he said. "It's used as a diuretic."

"What's that mean?" Matt asked.

"It means it makes you have to go to the bathroom rather frequently. It helps prevent headaches from altitude sickness, but you'll also notice the urge the use the bushes more often on our hike."

"No kidding," Matt said. "I didn't think I'd make it outside."

Just then we heard a sharp crack. A large black shape emerged from the bamboo forest. In the silvery gray of the moonlight we saw first one cape buffalo and then another. They began grazing on the grass.

"We'd better get back in, boys," Dr. Freedman said. "And if you have the urge again tonight, use the porch like we did this time. I don't want to have any of you walking into a buffalo."

My dad's radio alarm went off at 5 A.M. followed by the BBC news again. Matt groaned, "Man, what a night. I had to get up three times!"

None of us had slept too well. I sat up in my sleeping bag. I pulled my socks out of the bottom of my sleeping bag where I had stuffed them so they'd be warm in the morning. Then I got dressed. We had bananas and cold cereal for breakfast. Then we made sandwiches for our lunch on the path. My dad handed out oranges and chocolate bars as well. "Keep snacks handy," he said. "And be sure to carry water. We won't hit any streams until we reach the Teleki Valley. And you'll need plenty to drink—especially with these pills."

We stepped outside and found Francis and the others ready to leave. The two porters took our two heavier backpacks and weighed them on a hand-held hanging scale. They complained that the packs weighed too much and they'd have to charge us more. My dad immediately began pulling out some of the heavier items and putting them into his pack. Francis stopped him. "Don't do that," he said.

"Why not?" my father asked. "You said they're over the limit. Go ahead, try weighing them now."

"It's not a matter of weight," Francis said smiling. "It's a matter of money. For every pound over the limit we charge an extra ten shillings. My men can easily carry the packs. But it's the system to allow the porters to make more money."

Dr. Freedman looked annoyed and he said, "Let's carry the extra weight. They can't blackmail us for more money."

But Dad had a gentler approach. "Ten shillings per pound really isn't too much," he said. "And these porters only get four or five dollars a day for their work. Let's go with the system and let them carry the weight."

The porters smiled happily and agreed to the extra pay. Then they effortlessly tossed their own rucksacks on top of the backpacks and tied everything together with sisal string. We set off up the mountain, the sun creating diamonds on the dew-covered grass.

The first hour the path wound through trees and thick bamboo. Then the trees thinned out. Francis had us stop to rest on a rock next to a wooden post that had been painted red and white.

"Are we getting near the North Pole?" Matt asked, trying to be funny.

His comment puzzled Francis. "These poles mark the path through the vertical bog. If you get lost, look for a red and white post."

"Tell us about the vertical bog," I asked Francis.

He looked up above us. "It starts here. Rain somehow funnels into this place and seeps out of the side of the mountain. So even though we are climbing a very steep section, it's wet and muddy. Water collects in muddy pools and grass grows in clumps around the water. So you'll have to try to keep on top of the grass or the rocks. Do your best not to step into the mud. It's knee-deep in places and if your boots get soaked it's hard to keep your feet warm as we go on up the mountain."

After we'd rested for about ten minutes, we set out to tackle the vertical bog. All the trees were below us now replaced by clumps of giant heather, big bushes that looked like sculpted Christmas trees. At first the bog was fun. "It's like a giant maze," I said to Dave as we zigged and zagged, trying to put our feet on the firmest places. But it got steeper. And boggier. My backpack seemed to have gone on a weight-gaining binge and the straps bit into my shoulders. I leaned against a boulder to catch my breath. Dave joined me.

"This is hard work," he said. I nodded.

Matt and Jon had moved off to the right, trying to find the drier spots. Suddenly Matt yelled, "Hey, there's an airplane over here!"

Francis, waiting for us to catch up, shouted down, "Yes, it crashed there last year. You can look around it if you like." Matt and Jon moved off.

"Let's join them," Dave said. He loved airplanes and had a secret dream of some day being a missionary pilot. Leaving our packs, we hurried over to join Matt and Jon. The airplane, painted red and white, had plowed into the moor grass and sheared off one wing. The windows had all been shattered.

Francis came over. "What happened?" Dave asked him.

Francis said the plane had flown too close to the mountain and had been sucked into the ground by a down draft. "All three people on board were killed," Francis said, answering our unspoken question.

"Come back to the path," he urged. "We have to keep climbing."

Collecting our packs, we climbed up to where Dad and Dr. Freedman had sat down to rest.

As we got near them, I stepped on a clump of grass that wobbled under my feet. I leaned backward and the weight of my pack pulled me off-balance. I took a quick step backwards to keep from landing flat on my back. One foot went knee-deep into a mud hole.

Dad ran over and grabbed my hand. With his help I pulled my foot out of the mud with a quiet sucking sound.

"Try to wipe off as much mud as possible on the grass. It should be okay," Dad said after examining my boot.

We continued to climb. The vertical bog finally gave way to rolling moorlands with occasional boulders. We stopped by one big rock to eat our lunch. Now we began seeing different kinds of lobelia plants. Dad pointed them out as we passed.

"That's the water-filled lobelia. It catches the dew and you can always get a drink. That one over there is the cabbage lobelia. It looks like a giant head of cabbage. And that feathery looking one is called the ostrich plume lobelia." He kept talking, which helped us forget our fatigue and aching shoulders. The path now led up a ridge above the Teleki Valley. Far below us a river rushed down from the icy glaciers at the top of the peaks. The clouds over Mt. Kenya parted briefly giving us a glimpse of the looming mountain we had set out to conquer.

We hiked down the ridge into the Teleki Valley. We leaped across the river and then stopped and filled our canteens with the clear mountain water.

"It's close now," Francis said. "But don't hurry. At this altitude it's best to take things slow."

We strolled up the valley stopping to look at the furry brown hyrax that ran out of their burrows in the rocks to see if we'd give them a snack.

We also met some Japanese climbers coming down the mountain. They couldn't speak English very well, but we understood that they'd climbed to the top. They smiled and nodded their heads and looked very happy. They gave each of us a candy to celebrate their victory. We thanked them. After they'd gone on down, I opened up my candy. It was a deep-brown square. I took a bite and almost gagged. It tasted like coffee grounds. I didn't like coffee and this was nasty. I tried to give it to the hyrax but they didn't want it either.

"Pick it up, Dean," Dad said. "The rule on the mountain is you have to pack out your own garbage." He shook open a small plastic bag he carried for carrying out garbage. I put the candy in the bag.

At last we reached Mackinder's Camp, a stone bunkhouse at the head of the Teleki Valley looking up at the peaks of Mt. Kenya. As we set down our packs and claimed bunks by laying out our sleeping bags, Dr. Freedman sat down abruptly. "Oh, my head!" he groaned as he rubbed his temples with his fingers.

chapter twelve

POINT LENANA

"Is it the altitude?" my dad asked.

Dr. Freedman nodded. "I think so." He breathed deeply. "My lungs feel fine." He placed his finger alongside his neck and counted his pulse rate. "My pulse is a little high, but that's to be expected. It's just my head. It feels as heavy as a rock. And I can't move it without pain." He winced as he slouched on the bench.

"I'll get you something to ease the pain," Dad said, starting to rummage in his backpack.

"There's ibuprofen tablets in my medical kit," Dr. Freedman said.

My dad got the medicine for him and then helped Dr. Freedman lie down on a bunk.

"How are the rest of you feeling?" Dad asked.

Dave said his stomach felt queasy. But the rest of us felt pretty good. "Well, have a look around outside for a while. Then come back in and help me with supper. We'll eat early and go to bed. Remember, we're going to wake up at 2:30 in the morning so we can get to the top by sunrise."

The thin air was chilly even with the late afternoon sun. We looked up at the peaks of Mt. Kenya standing above us like proud soldiers. Francis and some of the porters lounged on the ground, enjoying the sunshine.

"What's that peak that sticks out like a knife?" I asked. "It looks so much taller than the others."

Francis laughed. "That's Point John. It only looks bigger because we're right under it. By tomorrow morning you'll be looking down at that place." He pointed out our route along the scree and then up the side of Lewis Glacier. "From here you can't see Point Lenana," he said. "It's on the back side."

My dad called for us to bring some water so he could boil soup and *chai*. I carried the pot over to a pipe near the bunkhouse which poured out cold spring water. It had no faucet. The water just kept coming out and then ran away in a small ditch to join the river on the valley floor. I looked up at the ridge above us covered with giant lobelia plants, their long shaggy stems and large cabbage-like heads giving them the appearance of aliens from a science fiction movie.

Dad came out carrying his camera. "You can carry the water in and set it on the cookstove to boil," he said. "I've set up the cookstove on the table inside the door."

Then he knelt to take some pictures of the giant lobelias framing the peaks of Mt. Kenya.

None of us felt very hungry at supper, but Dad made us eat. He brought some soup to Dr. Freedman.

As we settled into our sleeping bags, my dad prayed with us. He also prayed for Dr. Freedman. Some other climbers in the room — there were over twenty bunks in the room — looked at us strangely as we prayed.

But one man, who said he came from Holland, asked why we prayed, and my dad had a chance to explain our faith in Jesus. The man, who was climbing the mountain with his girlfriend, said we'd given him something to think about.

As Dad set the alarm, he gave us one final piece of advice. "When you wake up in the night the most important thing will be to keep your feet warm so you should put your boots and socks in the sleeping bag with you. This room has no heat and it will be cold. Whatever you do, don't put your bare feet on the floor. And I'm not just worried about your comfort. Frostbite is a real possibility."

I thought of my muddy boots. I wasn't sure I wanted them in my sleeping bag with me. But I didn't want to lose any toes, either.

I didn't sleep well. The altitude sickness medicine woke me up about midnight. I had to drag on my warm clothes and my boots, get out of the bunk and struggle through the icy wind to the outhouse. Once back in bed, I was wide awake. I tried reviewing some of the verses I'd learned from Colossians and finally nodded off to sleep.

Then Dad shook me. "Time to get up," he whispered. Some of the other climbers in the room were also stirring. I shivered, then sat up and dressed while still in my sleeping bag. I wore thermal underwear and woolen army pants. I put on three pairs of socks and my boots. I pulled on several shirts and sweaters. On top of this I wore my down jacket and pulled on a stocking cap with "San Francisco 49ers" on the front. The other guys had similar layers of clothing. We had to be warm now. But as the sun came out we would need to take off layers of clothing.

We drank tea and ate granola bars Matt's mom had sent. Dad handed each of us some bags of homemade gorp as well as oranges and small boxes of juice.

"You don't have to carry your packs now," he reminded us. "We'll be up to the top and back here by mid-morning. But you'll need some snacks for energy on the way."

Dr. Freedman stumbled into the hallway. "How are you feeling, Dad?" Jon asked.

Dr. Freedman tussled Jon's hair. "Better," he said. "But I don't think I'll climb." He sat down at the table looking pale in the lamplight. "It feels like my body is adjusting to the altitude. But it would be foolish to climb higher. I wanted to see you off."

The Dutchman and his girlfriend waved as they headed out the door with their guide. "See you at the top," the man said cheerily.

Francis came to see if we were ready. Then he asked my dad if we had an extra flashlight he could use. His batteries had died. "He can use mine," Dr. Freedman said. He asked Jon to dig it out of his backpack.

We walked out into the raw wind that came screaming down the mountain. We hiked behind Francis in single file. Our second guide followed behind us. Francis walked in a slow, rolling walk. We followed, stopping to rest every twenty minutes or so. Soon we came to a place where small streams blocked our path. "Go carefully," Francis said. "You don't want to climb with wet feet."

We stepped gingerly on ice-covered stepping stones. Dave

stepped on one, and as he pushed off to reach the path on the other side, his foot slipped. He would have fallen in if Francis hadn't reached down and tugged him over the stream.

"Don't step on that rock," Francis said, moving downstream a bit and then pointing out a better way across.

After threading our way through the streams we came to a steep climb through gravel that had fallen off the mountain. Because of the steepness, we had to zig-zag our way up. Francis trudged up the mountain, stamping his toes into the loose gravel to get a grip. We followed like robots.

My legs ached. I couldn't get enough air to breathe. I sat down thankfully with my back against a boulder when Francis told us we could rest.

"I'm feeling sick," Dave announced. Then he stepped behind the rock and threw up. He came back, wiping the side of his mouth with his coat sleeve.

"Will you be okay?" my dad asked. He looked at Dave in sympathy.

"Yeah," Dave answered. "I feel a lot better now."

We continued to climb. Point John, looking like a shadow to our left, began to get smaller as we hiked above it. Francis told us that the dark area below Point John was a tarn, or alpine lake, at the bottom of Lewis Glacier.

As we rested, we heard voices and saw a flashlight coming down the slope. It was the Dutchman. "We can't make it," he said. "My girlfriend has a terrible headache from the altitude." We could see she was crying. Their guide nodded at Francis and then led them on down the mountain.

Near the top I felt so exhausted I thought I'd never make it. "Short rests," Francis commanded, pulling us to our feet after less than a minute. I think he knew we might not get going again if we rested longer. But we only took about twenty steps before he told us to take another short rest.

Dad had dropped back next to me. "How you doing, Dean?" he asked.

I looked up at him desperately. "I don't know if I can make it, Dad."

"See those rocks ahead?" he asked.

I looked at the rocks not more than twenty yards away and nodded.

"Just that far and you can rest again."

By setting my mind on short distances, I managed to keep going. Finally the path leveled out some and we saw a wooden hut ahead.

"Austrian Hut," Francis said. "It's where people who use ropes to climb to the highest peaks spend the night. We can go in and warm up. From here it's only half an hour to the top of Point Lenana."

We stepped into the Austrian Hut. It was crowded with other climbers. Some, like us, were just on the way to Point Lenana. Others would climb Nelion or Batian. We spent about twenty minutes resting and getting warm. Even though the cabin had no heat, at least we were shielded from the blast of wind from the glacier.

I ate some of my orange. Dave turned away quickly and said he didn't even want to smell food. Then Francis stood up and said, "Let's go."

The sun had started pinking the horizon to the east. We walked in the rosy light along the edge of Lewis Glacier. Mostly we walked on a rocky path. But toward the end we had to walk right across the ice itself. Someone had chipped out footholds so we put our feet in them and climbed slowly. We didn't have any extra breath for talking.

Then Francis stood in front of us smiling. "Pull yourself over this rock," he said. His back was against a six-foot cliff. We found some cracks and pulled ourselves over. We had reached Point Lenana! A metal cross stood on top of a jumbled pile of rocks that had been painted to look like snow. We walked over to the cross. My dad pulled out his camera to take our picture. We all waved and smiled. My dad had to take his woolen mittens off to work his camera. Before he was done, he started shaking his hand.

"What's wrong, Dad?" I asked.

"I can't feel my fingers," he said. "That wind sure makes it cold!" He stuck his hand back into his mitten to warm it before taking any more pictures. We could see the sun sliding up over the eastern horizon. Far to the south we could see the snow-coned top of Mt. Kilimanjaro, the only mountain in Africa taller than Mt. Kenya. A series of tarns laced the northern slopes like a string of pearls. We could look in all directions and see for forty miles or more. It was magnificent.

But the icy wind had made my nose numb.

"I'm glad we made it," Matt said, shivering. "Now I want to get back down. I'm freezing!"

"Me too," said Jon.

Dave had taken out his red Swiss army knife and was trying to scratch his name onto the painted concrete barrel provided for that purpose. But he finally gave up after carving a few crooked lines. "My hands are just too cold," he said.

"I'll get you all copies of my pictures," my dad said. "That will prove you made it to the top." Then he asked Francis to lead us back down.

At the Austrian Hut we saw an ice cave at a place where the Lewis Glacier dripped over. The sun had begun to warm up the air and the wind had died down. "Let's explore it," Matt said.

He and Jon slipped along down the snow to the ice cave. Dave said he didn't feel like going anywhere but home. I sat down to keep him company.

Soon Jon and Matt raced back up carrying ice spears. "Anyone want an icicle?" Matt asked. "We pulled them off the door of the cave. Man, it was blue in there."

Dave took an icicle and began sucking on it.

I glanced up at the Austrian Hut. I saw Francis and our other guide talking quietly with guides who had just come over the ridge leading up from the Chogoria side. They talked earnestly. Then I saw a Chogoria guide take out a bundle of green twigs which Francis slipped into his huge coat pocket.

"Dad," I said, "it looks like our guides are buying *miraa*."

"I'm not surprised," my dad said. "*Miraa* trees only grow on the north slopes of the mountain near Meru and it's quite an industry. The guides from Chogoria probably sell it to make extra money."

"But isn't *miraa* a drug?" I asked.

"It is, but since it's a local drug that's been used for years, it's not illegal in Kenya to buy it or sell it."

I wanted to tell him about my idea that *miraa* might have something to do with the break-ins at Rugendo. But just then Francis waved for us to start walking again. And I was too exhausted to talk anymore.

The trail looked a lot steeper going down. Loose gravel slipped under our feet and we had to bend our knees to keep from falling. Then Matt discovered that if you walked on your heels you could get going pretty fast and slip-slide your way down.

"Watch this," Matt said, and he started running, skidding to a stop next to a boulder.

"Looks like fun," Jon called and copied Matt. But after about six giant leaps, Jon lost his balance and began tumbling down the slope!

DOWN THE MOUNTAIN

I was so stunned by the sight of Jon falling boots-over-stocking cap that I couldn't move. He almost looked like our soccer ball when someone kicked it too far and it bounced down our steep dirt driveway. Francis was already running toward him. Jon did one more flip and landed in a deep pile of gravel that had built up next to a boulder. He stopped rolling and lay still.

Francis reached him and turned him over. Even from where I stood I could see the red stain on his forehead. Soon we had all gathered around. Jon sat up and held his hand to his head. "The cut's not very deep," my dad said, pulling out a small emergency medical kit from his camera bag. "I don't think it will need stitches." He took out several Band-Aids

107

that he'd carried in case anyone had blisters and placed three across the two-inch gash to draw it together. The bleeding stopped.

Jon shivered. "Boy, that was scary," he said.

"Do you hurt anywhere else?" Dad asked. He examined Jon's arms and legs for any broken bones and bruises. Satisfied that the injuries weren't serious, he told Jon to get up.

Jon stood up slowly, uncoiling like our cat, Pete, does after a nap. "I think I'm all right," he said. "I just feel kind of shaky."

We looked down the other side of the boulder and saw a drop-off of several hundred feet down toward the tarn. Dad said, "I feel a little shaky, too. You could have gone over the edge." Then he led us in prayer.

"Now, no more running," he said, and we continued our descent. Francis stayed close to Jon. By the bottom my legs felt like jelly from walking down at that steep angle. Dad complained that his knees hurt and he had started limping. We rested and then kept going, arriving back at Mackinder's Camp at about 10 A.M. Jon said his head ached.

"I'm going to have your dad check you out," Dad said to Jon. But when he went in he couldn't find Dr. Freedman anywhere. One of our porters appeared from behind the building and said Jon's dad had gone down the mountain with the Dutch couple because the woman had started having difficulty breathing.

"I hope they're all right," Dad said. "Let me have a look at you, Jon." He squinted as he examined Jon's eyes. "Hmm, your pupils are dilated normally."

"What's that mean?" I asked.

He explained. "After a bump on the head, often one of the

pupils will be very narrow. I think Jon will be okay. But the sooner we get him down to a lower altitude, the better."

Then Dad made us drink tea and eat more granola bars before we set off down the mountain. Francis offered to carry Jon's backpack for him. I felt better with every step down the mountain. So did Dave. "My stomach is starting to feel normal again," he said at a rest stop. He even opened a Cadbury's Fruit and Nut chocolate bar and ate it.

The vertical bog was just as slippery on the way down. Being in a hurry and not so concerned about wet feet, we slipped in more. Soon, I didn't care at all and sloshed straight through, leaving mud stains above the sock line on my legs.

My dad's knees started hurting again on the vertical bog and he fell behind as he tried to ease himself down without jolting them.

It was getting late as we walked into the Met Station. We saw Jon's dad lying on the grass with his head on his backpack. Jon ran over to him. "What happened to your head, Jon?" Dr. Freedman asked when he saw the bandages.

Jon told him about his fall. Dr. Freedman's eyes grew wide at the story. "Well, praise the Lord you're safe," he said. Then he gave Jon a brief exam and concluded that Jon hadn't suffered a concussion. The Band-Aids had pulled the cut together so it didn't need any stitches.

He gave Jon a gorilla hug.

"What happened to the Dutch couple?" my dad asked.

"They're okay," Dr. Freedman answered. "She was suffering badly from the altitude, but climbed anyway. The headache got too much for her and she cried so hard it set off an asthma attack. I knew the best thing was to get her to a lower altitude quickly. By the time we'd gotten half way down to the Met Station her headache had eased and she was breathing normally. They drove off in their Suzuki jeep and I think she'll be fine."

We loaded everything into our Land Rover. "Hey," my dad said as he opened his door. "What happened to my side mirror?" It had been wrenched off and the cracked mirror had been set on the windshield.

The camp manager came over. "We're very sorry, *Bwana* (sir)," he said. "Some monkeys came from the forest and started playing with your mirror. We thought it was funny but then two monkeys began to fight and one pulled it off. We chased them away and put your mirror back."

We could see muddy monkey footprints all over the hood. Dad shook his head. "I can't believe it! Monkeys broke the mirror. Oh well. Get in and let's go."

We bounced down the mountain, stopping to let Francis and the others out along the road. We thanked them for their help and our dads paid them a little extra and they waved good-bye.

We drove on down to Naro Moru River Lodge where we had booked a cabin for the night. After Dad picked up the key, we carried our packs to the porch and then pulled off our mud-caked boots and socks and went inside. We took showers in turn and put on clean clothes.

"Now, tonight, as a celebration, we're all going to eat at the hotel restaurant," my dad announced. We all cheered. Supper wasn't served until 7 P.M. so we sat down to wait for half an hour. Normally we'd have been using the last available sunlight to explore the Naro Moru River in front of our cabin. But we were all too tired.

The dining hall served a fancy six-course meal, but after

the main dish — some kind of chicken — my eyes began to get bleary. Across the table, Jon nodded off to sleep, jerking awake whenever someone spoke loudly. The waiter came and took away our plates. Matt yawned. My dad laughed. "I think you boys had better get to bed."

We walked back to the cabin and fell asleep as soon as we laid down. We never heard our dads come in later.

By the time we woke up the next day it was almost 11 A.M. Dad nudged me. "Wake up, you guys," he said. "We have to be out of the cabin in a few minutes or we'll have to pay for an extra day."

We groaned and struggled out of bed. Dad said we could swim in the hotel pool for a bit. We'd eat lunch at the snack bar before heading home.

We packed the car and went over to the pool. On the way I asked Dad if we could buy a shirt at the gift shop and then put it on the wall of the hotel bar.

"I think that would be fine," he said. "We did all make it."

"Except for Dr. Freedman, but he's not a Rugendo Rhino," I said.

"I think it's a great idea," Matt said. "Do we have enough money to buy a shirt?" he asked Dave, our club treasurer.

Dave assured him we did but the money was back in our tree house at Rugendo. "I'll cover the cost," Dr. Freedman said.

We picked a light green shirt. It had a picture of Mt. Kenya on the front with the Naro Moru River Lodge name under it. On the back a message read: I climbed Point Lenana. We decided to write our message underneath those words. Even though I was the secretary, we asked Dave to write our names. We wanted other people to be able to read it. Dave wrote with a ball point pen, making big outlined let-ters. This is what the message said: The Rugendo Rhinos Club. We climbed together. We reached the top together. We came down together. December 29, 1995. Then he wrote: Psalm 133:1 "How good and pleasant it is when brothers live together in unity!"

Underneath this he wrote our names: Matt Chadwick, Dean Sandler, Jon Freedman, Dave Krenden.

"That looks great," Matt said.

"Now each of you put your signature under your name," Dave said.

I scrawled my name on the shirt.

We went to the bartender who pinned our shirt up on the wall with thumbtacks.

After our swim and lunch we drove back to Rugendo. As soon as we drove up to Jon's house, Mrs. Freedman came running out calling for her husband. "They need you at the hospital right away! Robbers broke into Mr. Macheru's house in the middle of the night and beat him with a club before stealing his TV and other things. They helped him as best they could, but he's still unconscious and they need your advice."

chapter fourteen

THE CULPRIT IS CAUGHT

The bad news tarnished the joy of announcing that we had made it to the top of the mountain. We dropped off Jon and Dave. At Matt's house, Mr. Chadwick and my dad talked about the break-in.

"I thought the burglaries had settled down," Dad said. "I was even considering calling off the night patrols."

"I just don't know what else we can do," Mr. Chadwick said. "Last night's attack on Mr. Macheru, the high school headmaster, was quite brutal."

"We'll have to keep praying that God will protect all of us here at Rugendo. And pray he'll reveal who's behind all the burglaries," Dad said.

That night the missionaries and church leaders held

another prayer meeting. When my parents came home they told me Mr. Macheru had regained consciousness. He'd suffered a concussion, but it looked like he would recover completely.

Then Mom told me that on my birthday they would have a special party for me. They would invite not only my friends but also my teachers and then show them what I'd accomplished with my Twelve Tasks of Manhood. It would be a time to tell everyone I'd left childhood behind.

"I'd rather just have the Rhinos over, Mom," I said.

"I know," she answered. "But it's important for others to know what you've done. You're going to be a man."

Tears bubbled up in her eyes as she gave me a hug.

I asked if I could invite Kamau. "Sure you can," my mom said. "You can show him that you're becoming a man, too. I heard that all the boys who went to that circumcision camp came back yesterday."

The next morning I told the Rhinos about my party.

"What kind of cake will your mom make this year?" Matt asked. "She always makes such neat cakes. Remember last year's rocket cake that burned down the stump? And the soccer ball cake the year before? And the best part is all the thick frosting. I love your mom's cakes."

"I'm not sure," I said. "She said she might try to make a Mt. Kenya cake."

"That would be great!" Jon said.

"I'm going to ask Kamau to my party," I said. "Do you guys want to come?"

We found Kamau with some goats near the muddy brown stream that ran by Rugendo. When he saw us he turned away. I walked over to him. "Hello, Kamau," I said. He still refused to look at me.

"I hear all the boys have come back from circumcision camp," I said, trying to make conversation, but puzzled by Kamau's silence. "How does it feel to be a man?"

Kamau didn't answer.

"Did I do something wrong?" I asked. "I just wanted to invite you to my birthday party next week. Remember how I got that book last year with all the tasks I had to complete before my thirteenth birthday? Well, by climbing Mt. Kenya I've done all but one. That last task will be fun. It's eating a *nyama choma* (roast meat) dinner in Nairobi with my dad the night before my birthday. Anyway, since you came to my last birthday party, I thought you'd like to come to this party and see me as I become a man."

Kamau looked at me sadly and shook his head slowly.

"Forget him," Matt said. "He doesn't want to come. Maybe since he's now a real man he's not allowed to talk with kids like us. Let's go home."

I tried one last time. "I'd like you to come, Kamau. You're my friend."

Kamau turned his back on me. So we walked away. "I don't understand what's wrong with Kamau," I said.

We stopped off at the *chai* house for some *chai* and *mandazi*. As we soaked the square doughnuts in our *chai*, a young boy with a torn pair of shorts poked his head around the door. Seeing us, he walked over and handed me a folded piece of paper. I opened it. It read: Meet me at 2 P.M. at the waterfalls. It was signed by Kamau.

"What do you think of this note?" I asked the others as we walked home.

"I have no idea," Matt said. "But we should go to the waterfalls and find out."

That afternoon we hiked to the falls and sat on the mist-slick rocks and waited. Two o'clock came and went. "I'm going swimming," said Matt, slipping his shirt and shorts off. Wearing only his underwear, he jumped into the pool under the falls. We joined him, splashing and yelling.

Suddenly I noticed Kamau sitting by the side of the pool. We hurriedly climbed out and dressed. Kamau still looked sad. "I have a big problem," he said. "I didn't know who to tell. But when you tried so hard to be friends with me this morning, I decided I had better tell you."

We sat down to listen. "Last week I was so happy," Kamau said. "I endured the circumcision operation bravely. I had been with other boys my age learning about the Lord. We committed ourselves to follow Christ and to stand as soldiers of God and bring our nation, Kenya, to Christ. I had healed from the surgery. And all of us boys from the Rugendo area came home two days ago. My parents welcomed me back. They proudly told all the neighbors that their son had become a man."

"So what's the problem?" Matt said. "Sounds pretty good."

"I'm getting there," Kamau said, refusing to be rushed by Matt who always liked to read the last chapter of a Hardy Boys mystery first so he'd know what was going to happen. "The day we came back I was invited to a celebration for all the newly circumcised boys. My parents hadn't heard about it, but they said I could go. I was a man, now. So I went..."

Kamau's voice trailed to a stop. "What happened?" I asked.

Kamau shook his head as if trying to forget some bad

dream. "There was a man there who called himself Munene," Kamau continued. "He told us he had called the party and was roasting a goat in our honor. Then as we ate, Munene told us that he was going to introduce us to some of the pleasures of manhood. He pulled out some *miraa* and told us how to chew it. He said it would make us feel brave and bold. I only pretended to chew. But as the evening went on, the other boys chewed more and more. Soon another group of boys came who had been circumcised last year. They encouraged us to keep chewing *miraa*.

"Then Munene talked about how unfair it was that the missionaries had so many nice things. He told us we had to prove our manhood. We would break into the headmaster's house that night and steal his TV. We would then sell it and share the money. It wouldn't really be stealing, Munene told us. The headmaster had grown fat on the school fees of hard working parents just as the missionaries had grown rich living on Kikuyu land.

"I knew he was saying bad things, but I was too afraid to speak up. I didn't want the others to think I wasn't a real man. The other boys got angrier and angrier. I think the *miraa* made them act crazy. By the middle of the night, Munene led us to Mr. Macheru's house. I stayed outside and kept watch while the others broke down the door and beat up Mr. Macheru. They came out with the TV and some other things."

Kamau stopped. Then he said, "It was terrible. When I heard Mr. Macheru was in the hospital my stomach turned. What if he died? If the others knew I told you I think they'd kill me."

We sat silently. Finally I said, "You did the right thing,

Kamau. I think my dad and Pastor Waweru can investigate Munene without anyone knowing you're the one who told."

Kamau put his hand on my shoulder. "I had to tell someone. Now I must go. Please don't tell anyone I was the one."

After Kamau had slipped away we Rhinos ran back to Rugendo. Without revealing Kamau's name we told my dad all about Munene and the *miraa* connection. Dad got Pastor Waweru and Mr. Chadwick and they went to the police.

That evening Dad said the police had arrested Munene. They'd found Mr. Macheru's TV set in his house. "Munene moved near Rugendo a little over a year ago and started selling *miraa*. Then, just as you boys said, he gave it free to some teens who had recently been circumcised. Munene got the boys all worked up and then led them to burglarize houses. That's why the stealing stopped for awhile. He'd just gotten hold of this year's circumcision group so the raids began again. Munene gave the police a list of all his accomplices."

"What's going to happen to the teenagers who did the robbing with him?" I asked.

"Pastor Waweru is going to tell all the parents what happened. For now they are just being warned. The police feel that without Munene's pressure and *miraa*, most of the young men won't steal anymore. I went with Pastor Waweru when he talked to the first few parents, and their boys were glad that Munene had been caught."

He looked at me. "The boy who seemed most relieved was Kamau. I thought you'd like to know nothing will happen to him."

I don't know how Dad figured out it must have been Kamau who had told us about Munene. But I smiled. "I'm really happy for Kamau," I said.

"Did the police find any of my clothes?" Mom asked.

"I'm afraid not," Dad answered. "Munene sold all the stolen goods in Nairobi. And the young men said he never gave them any of the money so they'll be happy to testify against him in court. He didn't have a chance to sell Mr. Macheru's TV or the police wouldn't have any evidence."

We Rhinos went over to Matt's house that evening to watch a video and eat popcorn. "Wasn't that great how we helped solve the mystery of the break-ins at Rugendo?" Matt boasted.

"Well, really it was Kamau," I said. "We suspected *miraa* had something to do with it, but we didn't know who was doing the stealing. Not until Kamau took the risk and told us what he'd seen."

"Yeah, you're right," Matt said. "Anyway, I'm glad Munene's in jail."

Just then we heard a loud bang against the window.

chapter fifteen

A MAN-SIZED
BARBECUE

Matt jumped away from the window. "Burglars!" he
yelled.

Mr. Chadwick ran out of his bedroom. "What's going on?"
he asked.

"We heard someone at my window," Matt said. "I'm sure
it's a burglar."

Mr. Chadwick grabbed his Maasai spear and flashlight
and cautiously stepped out of the house. Then he laughed.
"Come here, boys," he said. "Here's your burglar."

"A quail!" Jon said, bending down and picking up the
small bird. It had flown right into the window and now,
dazed, it didn't know where to go. Soon we heard more
thuds as quails hit the roof of the house.

We spent the next half hour collecting quails.

"Not as many as God sent to the children of Israel," Mr. Chadwick said. "They must be migrating through the area. Remember, Matt, a few years ago when we caught several hundred?"

A few had been battered by their encounter with the house so we put them out of their misery and planned a quail roast the next day. We wanted to keep the others but Matt's cat eyed them hungrily so we released them.

"I'm sure glad it wasn't a burglar," Matt said.

"Me too," his dad answered. "Now maybe we men can get a good night's rest around here."

The next week my dad took me out to dinner at the Carnivore Restaurant in Nairobi. It was an all-the-meat-you-can-eat barbecue. We sat down at a small square table. In the middle of the restaurant a large circular barbecue pit roasted meat skewered on Maasai swords. The waiter brought us black cast-iron plates which were so hot that when I put butter on my plate for my roll, it melted. Then the waiters started bringing the meat. Putting the point of the sword on my plate, the waiter asked if I wanted *kongoni*. I nodded and he sliced off a big slab of antelope meat. Then came beef, ostrich, lamb, pork, buffalo, crocodile, chicken, sausages, barbecued pork ribs, and more. I ate until my eyes began to bulge out.

As we sat back and had ice cream for dessert my dad congratulated me on making it through all twelve tasks. "Tomorrow you turn thirteen," he said. "Now I know I've talked to you a few times about the proper way to treat a girl. But I also know that in the next few years a lot of older boys are going to feed you a lot of stories about sex. Most of what you hear will be false."

My face flushed and I could feel my ears heating up. He went on as if there wasn't another person in the world, let alone in that crowded restaurant. "So tonight I'm going to tell you again about God's gift of sex and the importance of staying pure until marriage. And if you ever have any questions, just come to me and we'll talk, man-to-man."

Then he launched into his talk. Looking wildly around the room I hissed, "Dad, please, not here!" He smiled and went on talking.

THE END

GLOSSARY

1. *Rungu* (ROO-ngoo) — A wooden club often used for hunting birds or as a weapon for self-defense. A *rungu* usually has a knob the size of a baseball on the end.

2. *Wazungu* (Wah-ZOO-ngoo) — The Swahili word for white people. The word literally means people who are always going around in circles. When the white people first came into East Africa they were exploring and would only set up temporary camps before moving on to some new place. So the Africans called these strange white people *Wazungu*.

3. *Twiga* (TWEE-guh) — The Swahili word for giraffe.

4. *Shilling* (SHILL-ing) — The basic unit of currency in Kenya is called a shilling. The British introduced shillings when Kenya was a British colony. A shilling is a silver coin a bit larger than a quarter. It takes about fifty shillings to make one U.S. dollar.

5. *Miraa* (Mee-RAH) — A kind of tree that grows on the northeastern slopes of Mt. Kenya. The leaves contain powerful narcotic alkaloids and people chew the leaves to make themselves feel strong or to stay awake. Farmers harvest the leaves which are tied in tight bundles and sold as a stimulant in Kenya, Somalia, and the Arabian Peninsula.

6. *Jembe* (JEM-bay) — A garden hoe. The *jembes* in Kenya are usually about six inches wide and ten inches long and have a rough wooden handle. Kenyan farmers use *jembes* to dig the soil before planting and to get rid of weeds around crops.

7. *Panga* PAW-nguh) — A big cutting knife used for clearing bush and cutting firewood. A *panga's* blade is about two feet long. The wooden handle is usually covered with tightly wrapped inner-tube rubber. The end of the blade on a *panga* is curved upwards like the front of a canoe.

8. *Matatu* (Maw-TAW-too) — A small bus or converted pickup used to carry passengers and luggage. The name comes from the Swahili word *tatu* meaning three. The first privately owned vehicles to carry passengers around the Nairobi area used to charge people three shillings each so the taxis became known as *matatus*.

9. *Mabati* (Maw-BAW-tee) — Corrugated metal roofing sheets that are used in Kenya on most of the houses. Each *mabati* sheet is about six feet long and three feet wide. The *mabati* roofs are usually very shiny and are used to collect rainwater for drinking.

10. *Chai* (CHAH-ee) — The word for tea in Swahili. *Chai* is made by boiling a mixture of milk and water in a pan over a fire. When it begins to boil tea leaves and sugar are mixed in and the *chai* is set aside for a few minutes. The *chai* is then

poured through a strainer. It is sweet and milky and, if cooked over a traditional cook fire, it has a smoky taste as well.

11. *Mandazi* (Muh-NDAH-zee) — The Swahili word for square African doughnuts without a hole in the middle. *Mandazi* are often served with tea for dunking.

12. *Chang'aa* (Shung-AH) — Traditional African beer made by fermenting sugar and some kind of grain, often millet. *Chang'aa* brewing is illegal so it is done secretly. The amount of alcohol in *chang'aa* varies a great deal and every year people die in Kenya from alcohol poisoning after drinking it.

13. *Irio* (EE-ree-oh) — In the Kikuyu language *irio* literally means any kind of food. But it has come to describe a staple dish among the Kikuyu — a mixture of mashed potatoes, kernels of corn, and pumpkin leaves. The pumpkin leaves make *irio* a bright green color.

14. *Rugby* (RUG-bee) — A sport that looks like a mix between soccer and American football. The sport started at Rugby School in England when a frustrated student, William Webb Ellis, picked up the ball in a soccer game and started running with it. In rugby you can carry the ball but you can only pass it backwards. A player carrying the ball can be tackled but no blocking is allowed. You can also kick the ball. Points are scored when a player carries the ball into the end zone and sets the ball down.

15. *Posho* (POH-shoh) — A porridge made with cornmeal and boiling water.

16. *Chapati* (Chaw-PAW-tee) — A *chapati* is a kind of fried flat bread. It is similar to a tortilla but thicker. Kenyans cook *chapatis* by making a dough from flour, water and salt.

The dough is rolled into a snake and oiled before it is coiled and rolled flat. As it fries on a hot iron skillet the *chapati* is smeared with oil on each side.

17. *Waterbuck* — A large antelope that never lives far away from water. The coat of the waterbuck is a kind of grizzled gray and it has a white ring across its rump as if it had sat on a toilet seat with wet white paint. The male waterbuck has heavy, ringed horns. The female has no horns.

18. *Reedbuck* — The reedbuck is a bright yellow-brown color. Three feet high at the shoulder, a reedbuck weighs 80 to 100 pounds. It lives in grassland near water and often hides in reeds along lakes or rivers. The horns of a reedbuck are short and go backward from its head before curling forward, almost like a parenthesis.

19. *Impala* (Im-PAW-luh) — A graceful orange-brown antelope. As they dance across the plains they have been known to make leaps of over thirty feet long and ten feet high. The male impala's horns are long (two to three feet) and gracefully curved like an S.

20. *Samosa* (Suh-MOH-suh) — A spicy fried pastry from India. A very thick pastry crust is rolled and stuffed with either spiced meat or vegetables. The spice mixture can be very hot. The pastry is then folded over the mixture in a triangle and fried in oil.

21. *Hyrax* (HIGH-racks) — A small rabbit-like animal that lives in rocky areas. Hyrax live in colonies of up to sixty in cliffs or among boulders on rocky hills. The coat of the hyrax is gray-brown. Their feet have rubber-like pads making it easy for them to climb steep slopes.

22. *Maasai* (MAW-sigh) — A tribe from East Africa. They are famous for keeping large herds of cattle and refusing to

change their traditional nomadic way of life. The women wear colorful beads while young warriors used to prove their manhood by killing a lion with a spear.

23. *Nyama choma* (NYAH-muh CHOH-muh) — *Nyama choma* literally means roast meat in Swahili. It is used to describe a barbecue where meat of any kind is roasted over a charcoal fire.

Pronunciation key for map

1. Mount Kilimanjaro (Kee-lee-maw-NJAH-ro)
2. Amboseli (Am-boh-SELL-ee) Game Park
3. Nairobi (High-ROH-bee)
4. Athi (AH-thee) River
5. Namanga (Juh-HAW-nguh)
6. Tanzania (Tan-zuh-NEE-uh)
7. Nyali (NYAH-lee) Bridge
8. Malindi (Muh-LIN-dee)
9. Kilifi (Kee-LEE-fee)
10. Mambrui (Mawm-BREW-ee)
11. Ngomeni (Ngoh-MEN-ee)
12. Garsen (GAR-sen)
13. Tana (TAW-nuh) River
14. Pate (PAW-tay)
15. Gedi (GEH-dee)
16. Wale (WAH-lay)
17. Mount Kenya (KEN-yuh)
18. Rugendo (Roo-GEN-doh)

Note: All the places on the map are real places except the mission station at Rugendo and the lost city of Wale, both of which are fictional places.